LUGHNASADH

GUIDE TO THE MAGIC OF THE SEASON
CELEBRATIONS OF OLD AND NEW
TRADITIONS
FOR THE SEASON OF THE HARVEST

ROBIN GINTHER VENNERI

KIPS Publishing
Rochester, Pennsylvania

LEGAL DISCLAIMER

We, KIPS Publishing, and the author Robin Ginther-Venneri are not herbal experts by any means and are not medical professionals. The products available, along with statements, opinions, views expressed, ideas, notes, procedures, and suggestions in this book, on the blog, on the website, in e-Books, on Facebook, Pinterest, and Twitter pages, and any follow-up comments on-site or by email, are opinions and are meant for informational purposes only. They are not meant to be used to diagnose, treat, prescribe, prevent, or cure any disease or to administer in any manner to any physical ailments. They are not intended as a substitute for the medical advice of a trained health professional. We cannot be held liable for your decisions and choices and the outcome of those decisions and choices. You are encouraged to do your own research and consult your healthcare professional before treating yourself or anyone else.

The information in this book, on the blog, on the website, in e-Books, on Facebook, Pinterest, and Twitter pages, and any follow-up comments on-site or by email is general and not specific to individuals and their circumstances. You must study herbs thoroughly and talk with a healthcare practitioner before you treat yourself or anyone else. I would like you to know that all matters regarding your health require medical supervision. Please consult your health care professional before adopting the statements, opinions, views expressed, ideas, notes, procedures, and suggestions in this book, on the website, in e-Books, on Facebook, Pinterest, and Twitter pages, and any follow-up comments on-site or by email, as well as about any condition that may require diagnosis or medical attention.

Herbs are very powerful, and if they are misused, they can be harmful. Herbs can also cause allergic reactions and interfere with traditional medications by blocking their effectiveness, increasing their effectiveness, or reacting with them harmfully. Always check with your health care professional before using herbs or herbal products!

Do not use herbal products of any kind if you are nursing, pregnant, taking medications, or undergoing treatment for any medical condition without consulting your health care professional.

Any plant substance, whether used as food or medicine, externally or internally, can cause an allergic reaction in some people. Neither KIPS Publishing nor the author Robin Ginther-Venneri can be held responsible for claims arising from the mistaken identity of any herbs or the use of any remedy or healing regime or because you did not first seek the advice of a trained healthcare professional as recommended. Do not try self-diagnosis or self-treatment for serious or long-term problems without consulting a healthcare professional. Do not undertake self-treatment while undergoing a prescribed course of medical treatment without seeking professional advice. Always seek medical advice if symptoms persist.

In addition, the statements made by the author regarding any products and/or services represent opinions alone. They do not constitute a recommendation or endorsement of any product or service by KIPS Publishing or the author. We, KIPS Publishing, and Robin Ginther-Venneri disclaim any liability arising directly or indirectly from using this book, on the website, on the blog, in e-Books, a class, class notes, follow-up email contacts, or of any products available or mentioned herein.

Additionally, the statements on the website, on the blog, in e-Books, on Facebook, Pinterest, and/or Twitter pages, and any follow-up comments on these sites or by email, have not been evaluated by the FDA. The information on this site is not intended to diagnose, treat, or cure any disease.

Thank you,
KIPS Publishing

Print ISBN: 979-8-9875591-5-4
First edition, 2023
KIPS Publishing LLC
Rochester, PA
www.kipspublishingllc.com

Everyone has a unique and awesome approach to their craft. What really counts is what speaks to you and moves your soul, regardless of what others do. I think it's subjective to each individual's interpretation of what they see, hear, and feel. My books cover the basics intending to provide you with a starting point for your own research or something new and engaging. I'm not perfect and don't have all the answers (if we're being honest), but every journey should involve learning and growth. As I continue researching, I'm learning alongside you, which I'm incredibly grateful for. So, I believe everyone is on their unique path to enlightenment, and you're not alone!

As always,
Blessings to You and Yours.

Contents

Acknowledgments..... 6
Wheel of the Year..... 7
Sabbat Dates..... 8
Sabbats: Wheel of the Year..... 9
The Wheel Explained..... 10
Quarter & Cross-Quarters..... 12
Witchcraft Paganism Wicca..... 13
Lughnasadh at a Glance..... 14
Quicky Lughnasadh..... 15
Correspondence..... 16
Intro to Deities 18
Goddesses..... 19
Gods..... 21
Lughnasadh Around the World.....27
Phases of the Moon..... 29
Oh Crap, A Full Moon..... 30
The Moon and Lunacy..... 31
Moons of the Year..... 32
Days for Spells and Rituals..... 35
Days Explained..... 36
Times for Spells and Rituals..... 40
Astrological Signs..... 43
Magic of the Months..... 48
Intro to Tarot..... 49
Colors at First Glance..... 77
Auras..... 79
Ying/Yang Energy..... 82
Chakras Energy.....84
Chakras at a Glance..... 85
Chakra Symbols..... 86
12 Chakras..... 88
Grounding..... 89
Centering 93
Shielding..... 95

Self Healing Your Chakras..... 97
Using a Pendulum..... 98
Simplified Psychic Abilities..... 100
Types of Empaths..... 101
Archetypes..... 104
Witch Words..... 106
Spirituality..... 108
The Elements..... 109
Intro to Symbols..... 119
Evil Eye Colors..... 120
What is a Spirit Guide..... 123
Types of Spirit Guides..... 124
Animal Guides 126
Angels..... 134
Runes..... 135
Correspondence..... 137
Foraging Calendar 138
Herbs..... 139
Crystals..... 186
Grab and Go Combos..... 215
Magical Water 224
Intro to Oils 231
Intro to Spells..... 243
Manifestation..... 249
Warding..... 251
Banishing..... 253
Self Care and Reflections..... 260
Index..... 280
Witchy Services and Shops..... 282
Book Recommendations..... 287
App Recommendations..... 289

Acknowledgments

Wow! I can't express how grateful I am for all the amazing people God has brought into my life since beginning this journey a year ago.

Your love, friendship, kindness, and guidance have truly enriched my life. I feel so blessed to have you all in my circle.

Each of you holds a special place in my heart, and I wish nothing but the best for you in return. Thank you for being a part of my journey!

And as always,
Blessings to You and Yours
From Me and Mine.

Wheel of the Year

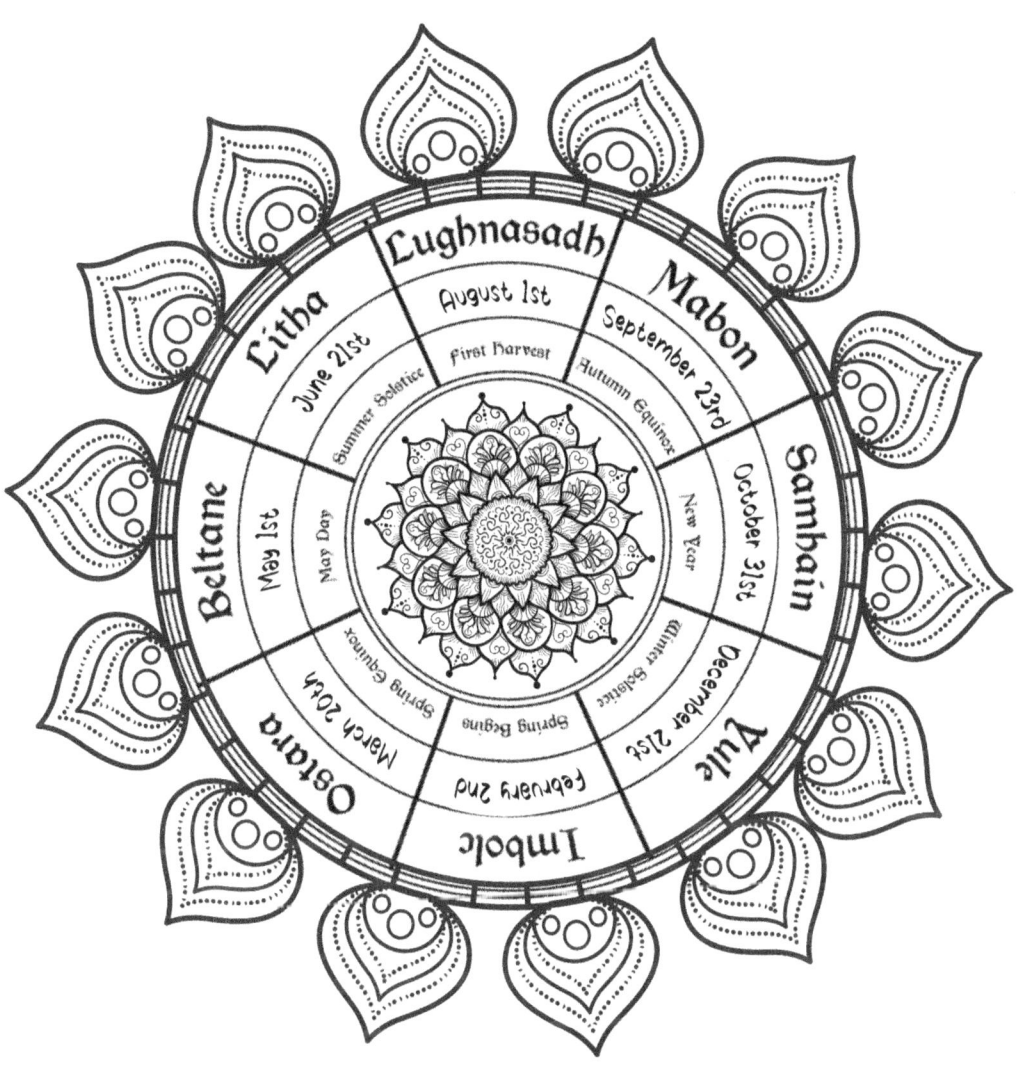

Sabbat Dates

Sabbat	Northern Hemisphere Date	Southern Hemisphere Date
Imbolc	February 1-2	August 1-2
Ostara	March 19-21	September 20-23
Beltane	May 1	October 31
Litha	June 20-22	December 20-23
Lammas	August 1-2	February 1-2
Mabon	September 21-24	March 20-22
Samhain	October 31	April 30
Yule	December 20-23	June 20-22

Sabbats: The Wheel of the Year

Yule - Winter Solstice
God as Oak King is born of the Goddess.
God as Holly King prepares to depart.
Goddess is the Mother of the Sun God.
Goddess is the Crone of Winter.

Imbolc - Purification and Fire
Goddess is cleansed and purified.
Milk flows for lambs and for the baby God.
The quickening of the Earth.
Goddess is preparing to return to Maiden.

Ostara - Spring Equinox
Goddess is Maiden/brings Spring.
God and Goddess encourage animal fertility.

Beltane - Fertility and Fire
God Youth and Goddess Maiden unite in love.
May Day flowers, romps, and bonfires.

Litha - Summer Solstice
God turns from Youth to Sage.
Marriage of God to Goddess.

Lughnasadh - Bread Harvest
God enters the Earth in marriage, giving his energy into the grain, now his body.
First Harvest/Bread Harvest-Grains.

Mabon - Autumn Equinox
God gives his spirit into the vines, fruit, and barleycorn;
wine, cider, whiskey, beer, and mead are now his blood.
He rules Underworld.
Goddess alone and pregnant with the God.

Samhain - Death and Rebirth
God within the Goddess, yet also Leader of the Wild Hunt.
The veil between the worlds at its thinnest,
Crone and Hunter [Lord of Shadows] reign together.

The Wheel of the Year Explained

The Wheel of the Year, or the Wheel of Life, represents the cycles of the Earth and life itself. It is how our ancestors marked the turning of the seasons and years, how farmers worked their land, and how we, as modern pagans, reconnect to the rhythms of the natural world.

The Wheel of the Year comprises eight holidays (i.e., holy days) or festivals. It is the cyclical calendar of the sun and moon, the natural world's rhythms.

Eight festivals are celebrated among those who follow the traditions of the sun and God and the Earth and Goddess. Four of these festivals are known as the Lesser Sabbats, linked to the sun. The other four, called the Grand Sabbats, are connected with the Earth.

The Lesser Sabbats are also called solar festivals, marking the two equinox solstices that occur each year. Equinox and solstice are related to the Earth's position in relation to the sun at a specific time.

During the equinoxes, the day and night are almost equal in length because the sun shines directly on the equator. On the other hand, the solstices are marked by the shortest day of the year (in June) and the longest day (in December), which are both influenced by the Earth's tilt.

The exact date varies each year by a margin of a few days. The Earth rotates around the sun in 365.25 days, and our calendar is set for 365 days. So we had a leap year every four years to the calendar to balance out.

These Lesser Sabbats are Yule, the Winter Solstice; Ostara, the Spring Equinox; Litha, the Midsummer Solstice and Mabon, the Autumn Equinox.

The seasonal festivals or Grand Sabbats mark the four significant season changes for the year. They are also referred to as cross-quarter days or fire festivals.

We mark this divide at the equinoxes. So the next dark half of the year starts with the Autumn Equinox (Mabon). The light half of the year begins with the Spring Equinox (Ostara).

The dark half of the year is about drawing inwards. After that, it is the cold, hibernating months when we go within to do inner work, contemplation, and meditation.

We use this time to rest and recoup after the busy, bustling energy of the light half of the year. We focus now on our home and hearth.

The light half of the year is about looking outwards. It is the warm, heady months of spring and summer. The sun is at full strength, and life abounds everywhere you look.

In the light half of the year, we work with our communities, traditionally planting the fields, tending the newborns, and gathering into pairing foods for the winter store. Births, weddings, harvest feasts, and general merriment abound.

The light half of the year begins with the Lesser Sabbat at the Spring Equinox, Ostara, in September. The Grand Sabbat of Beltane follows at the start of summer in October. Next on the way was the Lesser Sabbat at the Mid-summer Solstice, Litha, in December. Finally, Lughnasadh/Lammas is at the beginning of autumn in February.

That Wheel of the Year is based strongly on Celtic and other European cultures, but the symbology and concepts are found in many ancient cultures worldwide.

Quarter and Cross-Quarters

The eight seasonal festivals celebrated in Pagan and Wiccan traditions are divided into quarters and cross-quarters. The quarters, also known as the solstices and equinoxes, mark the four major points of the solar year, including Yule (winter solstice), Ostara (spring equinox), Litha (summer solstice), and Mabon (autumn equinox). On the other hand, the cross-quarter sabbats occur midway between the quarters and symbolize the shifting seasons, such as Imbolc (around February 1st), Beltane (around May 1st), Lughnasadh/Lammas (around August 1st), and Samhain (around October 31st). These cross-quarter sabbats hold spiritual significance and often commemorate the agricultural cycles or ancestral connections. Dividing the sabbats into quarters and cross-quarters provides a balanced representation of the changing seasons and the cyclical nature of life. While the quarters align with the solstices and equinoxes, emphasizing the sun's influence on the Earth, the cross-quarters highlight the subtle transitions between the seasons and the interconnectedness of all living beings, honoring the Earth's natural rhythms.

Quarters - Green [Lesser] Sabbats

Yule - Winter Solstice
God is born of the Goddess.
Goddess is both Mother and Crone of Winter.

Ostara - Spring Equinox
Goddess is Maiden/brings Spring to Earth.
God and Goddess encourage the fertility of Earth.

Litha - Summer Solstice
God turns from Youth to Sage/Oak to Holly King.
Marriage of God to Goddess.
Holly King impregnates Goddess with Oak King.

Mabon - Autumn Equinox
God gives his blood into the vines.
Goddess alone and pregnant with the God.

Cross-Quarters - White [Greater] Sabbats

Samhain - Death and Rebirth
God within the Goddess/tomb becomes the womb.
The veil between the worlds is thinnest.

Imbolc - Purification and Fire
Milk flows for the baby God as Oak King.
The quickening of the Earth.

Beltane - Fertility and Fire
God and Goddess unite in love.
May Day romps and bonfires/fertility encouraged.

Lughnasadh/Lammas - Bread Harvest
God enters the Earth in marriage, giving his body to be the grain.
First Harvest- grains.

Witchcraft Paganism Wicca

If you are new to magic and spirituality, distinguishing between Witchcraft, Paganism, and Wicca can be confusing. While some may use the terms Wicca and Witchcraft interchangeably, it is important to understand that they are not entirely the same. A Wiccan may be considered a Witch, but not all Witches are Wiccans. Additionally, while a Wiccan may identify as a Pagan, not all Pagans are Wiccans. Paganism refers to a group of polytheistic religions practiced before Christianity became widespread. The term "pagan" originally referred to rural villagers, but over time, it came to refer to those who continued to practice polytheism even after Christianity became dominant. Modern Paganism, also known as neo-paganism, encompasses a variety of spiritual beliefs and traditions. Wicca is one of these religions centered around the worship of a God and Goddess and a belief in reincarnation. It is characterized by a strong ethical code and specific rules that must be followed.

Not all Pagans follow the religion of Wicca, a neopagan religion. Wiccans are a type of Pagan who have chosen to follow Wicca, while other Neopagan religions include Druidism, Odinism, and shamanism. Despite their differences, these religions share common practices, such as celebrating Sabbats and using aids like herbs and crystals. Wiccans specifically believe in the concept of the One, which is the infinite source of everything and comprises the God and the Goddess - two opposite yet complementary energies that exist in everything. On the other hand, a Pagan may adhere to a different cult or possess their own spirituality without necessarily being part of the Wiccan religion. Other neopagan cults include Druidism, Odinism, and shamanism, which also celebrate Sabbats and use aids such as herbs and crystals. In conclusion, a Wiccan is someone who has consciously chosen to follow the cult of Wicca and believes in the One - the infinite source of everything composed of the God and the Goddess - two opposites that shape the energy that permeates everything.

Wiccan beliefs recognize the interconnectedness of life and death, emphasizing reincarnation as a new beginning rather than an end. It is a diverse religion with various streams, such as Gardnerian and Alexandrian Wicca, and is often confused with Witchcraft, which is a collection of practices and rituals. It's important to note that Witchcraft can be practiced by anyone, regardless of their religious beliefs. Witches, regardless of gender, can practice it with an open mind, and no specific religion is required, according to Scott Douglas Cunningham. While Wiccans belong to communities called "Covens," practitioners of Witchcraft typically work alone and do not feel obligated to bind themselves to deities.

One significant difference between the two is that Wicca follows the Law of Three, where everything we do comes back to us three times for good or evil. As a result, Wiccans do not practice Black Magic, believing that any harm inflicted will be returned three times over. However, Witchcraft does not have this limitation, and practitioners are guided by their conscience and common sense. The purpose of this guide is to provide a comprehensive overview of Witchcraft's world without imposing any spiritual or religious beliefs. The following chapter will delve into the specifics of magic potions and how they can enhance your life and the lives of those around you.

Lughnasadh at a Glance

Lughnasadh - August 1st

Northern Hemisphere: August 1st
Southern Hemisphere: February 1st
Pronounced: Lughnasadh or Lughnasa (pronounced LOO-nə-sə)
Themes: prosperity, gratitude, abundance, strength, growth, and protection

Also Known As Lugnasadh (Irish Gaelic "Assembly of Lugh"), Bron-Trogain (Irish Gaelic "Bringing forth [the fruits of] the earth"), Lunasda (Scots Gaelic), Lúnasa (Irish Gaelic), Lunasdal (Scots Gaelic), Luanistyn (Manx Gaelic), Gwyl Awst (Welsh "Feast of Augustus"), Lammas (English "Loaf mass"), Hlafmaess (Anglo-Saxon "Loaf mass"), Freyfaxi (Heathen), and Hlafmaest (Norse)

Observed by Historically: Gaels
Today: Irish people, Scottish people, Manx people, Celtic neopagans, Gallo-Roman religion, and Wiccans

Type: Cultural Pagan (Celtic polytheism, Celtic Neopaganism)
Significance: Beginning of the harvest season

Date: Sunset on July 31 – Sunset on August 1 (Northern Hemisphere)
Celebrations: The offering of First Fruits, feasting, handfasting, fairs, and athletic contests

Lughnasadh is a Gaelic festival marking the beginning of the harvest season that was historically observed throughout Ireland, Scotland, and the Isle of Man. Traditionally it was held on JJuly 31– August 1, or approximately halfway between the summer solstice and autumn equinox. Lughnasadh is one of the four Celtic seasonal festivals, along with Samhain, Imbolc, and Beltane. It corresponds to other European harvest festivals, such as the English Lammas.

There is no right or wrong way to celebrate any of the Sabbats. Pagans base their celebrations on cultural traditions, historical practices, and inclinations.

So live and let live!

Quicky Lughnasadh Correspondences

Archaeoastronomical Timing

The astronomical midpoint between the Summer Solstice and Autumn Equinox; Sun at 15 degrees Leo in the Northern Hemisphere and Sun at 15 degrees Aquarius in the Southern Hemisphere.

Some Pagans time the sabbat astronomically, while others celebrate on August 1, typically beginning at sundown on July 31 and ending at the next sunset. Other Pagans celebrate on August 5, called "Old Lammas" or "Old Style Lam-mas." Still, others time the sabbat per Nature's cues, celebrating when the wild berries become ripe or when the first crops of the harvest reach fruition.

Archetypes
Female
mother goddess
earth goddess
water goddess
water nymph
tree nymph
the pregnant mother
exhausted mother
selfless mother
the nurturer
the spirit of the land
the established queen

Male
father god
earth god
solar god
the warrior
the protector
the sacrificial god
the dying god
the spirit of vegetation
the newly crowned king

Heroes, Deities, and Goddesses
Tailtiu (Celtic)
Isis (Egyptian)
Dryads (Greek)
Demeter (Greek)
Kore (Greek)
Luannotar (Finnish)
Nemesis (Greek)
Ops (Roman)
Hathor (Egyptian)
Hecate (Greek)
Diana (Roman)
Pomona (Roman)
Juturna (Roman)
Stata Mater (Roman)
Danu (Celtic)
Artemis (Greek)

Heroes, Deities, and Gods
Osiris (Egyptian)
Lugh (Celtic)
Ganesha Chaturthi (Hindu)
Xiuhtecuhtli (Aztec)
Consus (Roman)
Thor (Norse)
Vulcan (Roman)
Thoth (Egyptian)
Loki (Norse)
Vertumnus (Roman)
Apollo (Roman)
Ragbod (Norse)

Quicky Lughnasadh Correspondences

Flowers
Marigold, sunflower, poppy, rose, aster, and cornflower

Trees
Apple, hazelnut, holly, and oak

Crystals
Citrine, topaz, carnelian, onyx, and quartz

Metals
Gold and brass

Incense
Cinnamon, apple, blackberry, marigold, and patchouli

Herbs
Blackberry, bilberry, basil, all spice, rosemary, garlic, bay, and fennel

Animals, Totems and Mythical Creatures
Lion, stag, eagle, dog and squirrel

Symbols and Tools
Corn dolly, Rowan cross, cornucopia, and pentacle

Food
Apples, corn, bread, squash, grains, nuts, berries, and potatoes

Drinks
Wine, mead, and apple cider

Colors
Yellow, brown, gold, and green

Activities and Traditions of Practice
Community fairs, reunions, gatherings, feasting, harvesting crops or wild herbs, making offerings to gods and ancestors, communicating with the dead, reflection and introspection, abundance magic, protection magic, sacrifice, games, competitions, expressing gratitude, and celebrating success

Acts of Service
Sharing food and other necessities with those in need, sprucing up neglected cemeteries, offering your time and energy to help another person ease their burdens or lighten their work-load, helping out at a community garden, doing yard work for elderly neighbors, providing social opportunities for those who are lonely or isolated.

Other Festivities During Lughnasadh

Alternate Names for Lughnasadh in Other Pagan Traditions

Lugnasadh (Irish Gaelic "Assembly of Lugh")

Bron-Trogain (Irish Gaelic "Bringing forth [the fruits of) the earth")

Lunasda (Scots Gaelic)

Lúnasa (Irish Gaelic)

Lunasdal (Scots Gaelic)

Luanistyn (Manx Gaelic)

Gwyl Awst (Welsh "Feast of Augustus")

Lammas (English "Loaf mass")

Hlafmaess (Anglo-Saxon "Loaf mass")

Freyfaxi (Heathen)

Hlafmaest (Norse)

Holidays or Traditions Occurring During Midsummer in the Northern Hemisphere:
Religious

Ghost Festival (Chinese, August, variable dates according to lunar calendar)

Festival of the Dryads (Grecian, August 1-3)

Nemoralia (Roman, August 13-15)

Lammas (Anglo-Saxon, August 1)

Tisha B'Av (Jewish, July or August, variable dates according to the lunar calendar)

Assumption Day (Christian, August 15)

Secular

National Aviation Day (United States, August 19)

Senior Citizens Day (United States, August 21)

Holidays or Traditions Occurring During Lughnasadh in the Southern Hemisphere:
Religious

Feast Day of Saint Brigit of Kildare (Catholic, February 1)

Candlemas, a.k.a The Presentation of Jesus at the Temple (Catholic, February 2)

Celebration of Yemanja (Candomblé, Brazil, February 2)

Nirvana Day (Mahayana Buddhist, February 8 or 15)

Lupercalia/Pan's Day (February 15)

Secular

Australia Day (Australia, January 26)

International Holocaust Remembrance Day (January 27)

World Wetlands Day (International, February 2)

Valentine's Day (February 14)

Chinese New Year (varies, late January to mid-February)

Introduction to Deities

Worshiping and dedicating to gods and goddesses is an important aspect of many pagan traditions, including those celebrating the Litha Sabbat. The honored and revered deities can vary greatly depending on the individual or group's beliefs and practices. Some may worship a pantheon of gods and goddesses, while others may focus their devotion on a single deity. Regardless of the approach, dedicating oneself to these powerful spiritual forces can be a significant and transformative experience.

Many pagans see their relationship with the divine as a two-way street. They believe they can receive blessings, guidance, and protection in return by offering devotion and reverence to the gods and goddesses. This energy exchange is often seen as a way to maintain balance in the world and one's life. Some also view the deities as archetypes or personifications of natural forces, such as the Sun or the Moon, and may seek to align themselves with these energies through worship.

There are many ways to worship and dedicate oneself to the gods and goddesses. Some may perform rituals or ceremonies, make food or drink offerings, or create sacred spaces in their homes or outdoor areas. Others may meditate, pray, or engage in personal acts of devotion. Whatever form it takes, this connection with the divine can be a source of inspiration, comfort, and spiritual growth for those who seek it.

Goddesses
Consus (Roman)

"He who gathers in." An ancient Roman divinity, whose name is derived by some from conso, i.e. consulo, while others regard it as a contraction of conditus. All we know about the nature of this divinity is limited to what may be inferred from the etymology of the name and from the rites and ceremonies which were observed at his festival, the Consualia. With regard to the former, some call him the god of secret deliberations, and others the hidden or mysterious god, that is, a god of the lower regions.

The story about the introduction of his worship throws no light upon the question since both explanations are equally in accordance with it. When after the building of Rome, the Romans had no women, it is said, and when their suit to obtain them from the neighboring tribes was rejected, Romulus spread a report that he had found the altar of an unknown god buried under the earth. The god was called Consus, and Romulus vowed sacrifices and a festival to him if he succeeded in the plan he devised to obtain wives for his Romans. Livy calls the god Neptunus Equestris. Hartung has pointed out reasons sufficient to show that Consus must be regarded as an infernal divinity; this notion is implied in the tradition of his altar being found under the earth and also in the fact that mules and horses, which were under the especial protection of the infernal divinities, were used in the races at the Consualia, and were treated with especial care and solemnity on that occasion.

Dryads (Greek)

Dryads, referred to sometimes as hamadryads in Greek mythology, are nature spirits that take the form of beautiful young women and live amongst tree branches. Their name comes from the ancient Greek word "drys," which means "oak"; however, later, all forms of tree nymphs were called dryads. These creatures have been said to be connected with their trees for life, existing only as long as the trees they inhabit.

Juturna (Roman)

Juturna was a prominent figure in ancient Roman mythology. Associated with fountains, wells, and springs, she had some auspicious connections; for example, she is said to have been the mother of Fontus by Janus. Moreover, it is believed that Jupiter transformed her into a Naiad (water nymph) and gave her two holy wells in Lavinium and Rome, respectively. Furthermore, at Ardea, an important cult was dedicated to healthful waters dedicated to Juturna. In addition, it is said that Castor and Pollux watered their horses from Juturna's sacred well after bringing news of the Roman victory at the Battle of Lake Regillus in 496 BC.

Kore/Persephone (Greek)

In Greek myth and religion, Persephone, also known as Kore or Cora, was the daughter of Demeter and Zeus. According to legend, she was later taken by her uncle Hades, the king of the underworld, as his queen. The myth surrounding her kidnapping has become symbolic of the seasonal agricultural cycle when crops are sowed at the start of wintertime and grow verdantly until their eventual harvest. Classical renditions usually depict Persephone wearing a robe with a big grain basket. However, many artwork images show her being forcefully whisked away by Hades himself.

The cult of Persephone and her mother, Demeter, was at the heart of the Eleusinian Mysteries, which gave hope of an afterlife to those who were initiated. Persephone's origins remain uncertain, but the cult likely stemmed from ancient agrarian beliefs. For example, anthesterion (the month of flower-bearing) in Athens was dedicated to her, while Epizephyrian Locris honored her as a goddess associated with marriage and childbirth. Known by many different names throughout history, including Proserpina and Libera in Latin cultures, she is also frequently compared to similar figures such as Attis, Adonis, and Osiris from other cultures. Additionally, variations on Persephone's narrative appear in Minoan Crete.

Gods
Loki (Norse)

Loki has been depicted throughout mythology and literature in many forms. Described as both mischievous and Machiavellian, he is said to have an "evil character" yet be "pleasing and handsome in appearance." His behavior is noted for its capriciousness and unpredictability; his loyalties are questionable - sources imply both a giant heritage as well as a romantic relationship with Odin. He often uses his cunning intellect to rescue gods from precarious situations, although he stands for evil on occasion. Loki can alter his form at will, taking the shape of a mare, flea, fly, falcon, seal, or old crone, amongst others. Tales of theft include Freyja's necklace and Thor's belt and iron gloves while also being credited unknowingly with birthing Odin's horse Sleipnir - Loki additionally allegedly sired the world serpent, Hel and Fenrir, who will devour the sun at Ragnarok. Little evidence exists which makes any connection between Loki and a fire god; this oft-cited claim may solely derive from the similarity of the name - logi meaning fire.

Luannotar/Luonotar (Finnish)

Titles: Daughter of Nature, Goddess of Creation, Water Mother, Sky Mother, was a virgin goddess of the air. Derived from the word ilma ("air") and -tar (the equivalent of English "-ress"), her name translates to Airress. She is also occasionally referred to as Luonnotar, which means "female spirit of nature" (in Finnish: luonto). Through Ilmatar, Väinämöinen, the main character in Kalevala, was born. This source of creation was memorialized by Jean Sibelius' tone poem Luonnotar (1913), which metaphorically highlights the birth of land and sky. The musical work brings to life two contrasting themes: shimmering possibilities and distressed cries emblematic of Ilmatar's tribulation-laden pregnancy.

Nemesis/Rhamnousia/Rhamnusia (Greek)

Nemesis: Greek goddess of vengeance. Nemesis is the goddess of indignation and revenge. Her name means "She Who Deals Out," she punishes those who experience undeserved happiness or excessive good luck. Nemesis hunts the wicked to distribute justice, and she is the force of karma within Greek society. Her symbols are the sword and the scales.

In Hesiod's Theogony, Nemesis is described as one of Nyx's children. However, various other Ancient Greek authors have attributed her parentage to Oceanus, Erebus, Zeus, and more. Similarly, numerous accounts suggest that Nemesis was the mother of Helen of Troy through Zeus. Finally, Tzetzes believed Nemesis had fathered the Telchines in conjunction with Tartarus.

Ragbod/Redbad (Norse)

Radbod (or Redbad), the last independent ruler of Frisia before Frankish rule, reigned in the area circa 680 until 719. He famously clashed with Charles Martel in the Battle of Cologne and was ultimately conquered by him. Although accounts vary as to what title Radbod held - kingship or ducal power - it is likely that when referring to their leaders, pagan followers observed them as kings, while Christianized Franks would have considered them dukes. His successors continued to fight against the Frankish rule for years after his death.

When Redbad came to power, succeeding King Aldgisl's rule and welcome of Christianity, he worked to free the Frisians from their Merovingian kingdom of the Franks by attempting to extirpate the religion. However, in 689, he was defeated by Pepin of Herstal at the Battle of Dorestand was forced to cede Frisia Citerior (Nearer Frisia) to the Franks. After Utrecht fell into Pepin's hands in 690-692, thereby giving them control over critical trading routes, Redbad made efforts to restore his power: fighting Charles Martel in Cologne in 716 and managing a marriage between Grimoald the Younger and Thiadsvind - Redbad's daughter - in 711. Eventually, though Charles prevailed and eventually overcame Redbad, who died in 719, his successors struggled against Frankish power for years following.

The story of Saint Boniface's unsuccessful attempt to convert Redbad has been passed down through history. According to legend, the ex-archbishop of Sens, Wulfram (or Vulfran), followed Saint Boniface on his second journey to Rome and attempted what would prove an unsuccessful bid to convert Redbad. Ultimately, when it was explained that upon death, he could expect no memory of his ancestors in Heaven, Redbad declared he intended, rather, to spend eternity in Hell with his pagan kin than Heaven with a pack of beggars. A similar version of this tale exists wherein bishop Willibrord replaces Wulfram.

Tailtiu (Celtic)

Tailtiu Goddess. Celtic (Irish). By tradition, the consort of Eochaid of the Tuatha de Danann, she is the foster mother of the god Lugh and is associated with the Lughnasad festival on August

Vertumnus (Roman)

Vertumnus is a Minor god of gardens and orchards. Roman. Of Etruscan origin, he is the consort of the goddess Pomona. Usually represented with garden implements and offered fruit and flowers. He was celebrated annually in the Vertumnalia festival on August 13.

Lughnasadh/Lammas

During Lughnasadh, which marks the major summer harvest, people express gratitude and celebrate with games and feasts. Also known as Lammas, this festival celebrates the first harvest, whether it's the first garden crops or plans that have come to fruition. Bread is often baked on this day to honor the grain harvest.

Lughnasadh is a significant festival for many Pagan faiths and is part of the Wheel of the Year. It begins at sunset on July 31 and ends at sunset on August 1, although it may extend to August 5 or 6 (known as Old Lammas or Old Style Lammas). The festival is also astrologically linked to when Leo completes a cycle with the sun's position, and it coincides with farmers beginning to reap their harvests. The day is referred to as Lunasda/Lunasdal in Ireland and Scotland, Luanistyn in the Isle of Man, and Gwyl Awst/Feast of Augustus in Wales. The English term "Lammas" comes from the Middle Ages phrase "hlafmaesse," which means "Loaf-mass."

Lughnasadh's name comes from the Celtic deity Lugh, who was originally associated with human skill, kingship, and protecting heroes. He was the king of Tuatha de Danaan, and with the help of the mother goddess Danu, he overthrew the previous rulers. He was also known for his craftsmanship and battle skills and later became linked to the Roman god Mercury.

Every August 1, many European cultures celebrate Lughnasadh (also known as Lunasa or Lammas) with bonfires, dancing, and other rituals. This ancient Celtic harvest festival is at least two thousand years old and honors the god Lugh. In Ireland, mountains and hills were traditionally climbed during this time, some of which became Christian pilgrimages. The Puck Fair in Killorglin, County Kerry, is also held each year around early August, where a wild goat is crowned "king" and a local girl is crowned "queen." Swiss people celebrate the national holiday with processionals, and Italians bless their fields on this day. Today, people continue to celebrate Lughnasadh with similar festivities in honor of the harvest.

Revival

Over the past few years, various cities in Ireland have initiated annual Lughnasa Festivals or Fairs. These festivities resemble Puck Fair and typically involve traditional music and dance, workshops, storytelling sessions, and markets. Some of these activities can be found in Gweedore or Brandon, while others are held elsewhere. Craggaunowen, an open-air museum in County Clare, organizes a yearly Lughnasa Festival where historical re-enactors portray daily life during the Gaelic period, showcasing clothing, artifacts, weapons, and jewelry. Similarly, Carrickfergus Castle in County Antrim hosts an annual event following the same model.

Neo-Paganism

Many Neopagan groups, including Celtic Neopagans, honor Lughnasadh and related rituals. How they celebrate can vary greatly; some strive to replicate the traditional festival as accurately as possible, while others incorporate a mix of influences, with the Gaelic version being just one of them. Generally, the event occurs once a year on July 31 to August 1 in the Northern Hemisphere and January 31 to February 1 in the Southern Hemisphere or during the full moon closest to these dates.

Wicca

Many Wiccans and Neopagans worldwide observe a Wheel of the Year with eight festivals. These celebrations, known as Sabbats, occur approximately every six months in both the Northern and Southern Hemispheres to correspond with local seasons. Lughnasadh, also called Lammas, is a notable event that marks the start of the autumn harvest and is considered an auspicious time for marriages or handfasting. It is preceded by Midsummer and followed by Mabon and Samhain. These Sabbats hold great significance for Wiccans.

Celtic Reconstructionism

During Lá Lúnasa, Celtic Reconstructionists express gratitude to the gods and goddesses for the beginning of the harvest season. They honor deities associated with powerful natural forces such as storms and lightning, seeking the protection of their crops through prayers and offerings to Lugh. The festival also celebrates Tailitu, who is invoked to keep the Cailleachan from harming the maturing crops. Traditionally, Gaelic followers celebrate either on "first fruits" or around the closest full moon. In North America, the festival coincides with blueberry harvesting in the Northeast or blackberry gathering in the Pacific Northwest.

Interesting History

The Romans celebrated Vulcan on August 23, the god of fire and volcanoes. They made sacrifices in hopes of protecting the city from devastating fires. Like the Greek god Hephaestus, Vulcan was renowned for his metalworking skills and was a god of the forge. Although he was somewhat deformed and portrayed as lame, as a son of Jupiter, he created his father's powerful lightning bolts and forged armor, weapons, and jewelry for the gods and heroes of Rome.

In English folklore, John Barleycorn is a symbolic character representing the crop of barley harvested each autumn. He also represents the wonderful drinks made from barley, such as beer and whiskey, and their effects. The traditional folksong, John Barleycorn, depicts the character of John Barleycorn's endurance of various indignities, which correspond to the cyclic nature of planting, growing, harvesting, and death.

Lammas, also known as Lughnasadh, has several myths and legends associated with it. One such story tells of Thor's wife, Sif, who had beautiful golden hair until Loki cut it off. Thor was angry and wanted to kill Loki, but some dwarves spun new hair for Sif, which grew magically as soon as it touched her head. The hair of Sif is connected to the harvest and the golden grain that grows every year.

Farmers in the Shetland Islands believed grain harvesting should only occur during a waning moon. They also thought this about the fall potato crop and peat cutting. At Lughnasadh, calves are weaned, and the first fruits, such as apples and grapes, are ripe. In some Irish counties, farmers believed they had to wait until Lughnasadh to start picking these fruits; otherwise, bad luck would befall the community.

In some countries, Lammas is celebrated with warrior games and mock battles, which may have originated from when people gathered to celebrate the harvest festival. Young men would showcase their strength and impress the girls by competing with each other. Artisans also offer their finest work in games and contests to honor Lugh, the mighty Celtic craftsman god.

It has become customary to gift a pair of gloves to people at Lammastide. This tradition began when landowners gave their tenants a pair of gloves after the harvest as a symbol of authority and benevolence. As winter is just around the corner, the gift of gloves is also practical.

During Lammastide, the fields are teeming with crops ripe for the picking. The late summer harvest is at its peak, and the first grains are being threshed while the apples hang plump on the trees. Gardens are overflowing with summer bounty, making this a time of great agricultural significance. Throughout ancient cultures, it has been a time of celebration and honor for the numerous gods and goddesses associated with this earliest harvest holiday.

Adonis (Assyrian)

The deity Adonis has a complex history with cultural influences from various regions. Despite being commonly depicted as Greek, Adonis originated from the early Assyrian religion. Adonis was worshipped as a god of the withering summer vegetation, and his mythos often includes a cycle of death and rebirth, similar to Attis and Tammuz.

Attis/Attys (Phrygian)

There are different versions of the story of Attis, a lover of Cybele, but all involve him castrating himself and eventually being transformed into a pine tree upon his death. Some sources suggest that Attis was in love with a Naiad and that Cybele, in a fit of jealousy, killed the tree where the Naiad lived, leading Attis to castrate himself out of despair. However, the common thread in all these tales is the idea of rebirth and regeneration.

Ceres (Roman)

Did you ever wonder why the crushed grains we eat for breakfast are called cereal? Interestingly, this name is derived from Ceres, the Roman goddess of harvest and grain. Moreover, Ceres was the one who taught humans how to preserve and prepare corn and grain after harvesting. She was regarded as a maternal goddess responsible for agricultural fertility in various regions.

Dagon (Semitic)

Dagon, a deity worshipped by the Amorites, an early Semitic tribe, was associated with fertility and agriculture. In early Sumerian texts, he was also referred to as a father-deity and sometimes depicted as a fish god. According to beliefs, Dagon bestowed the knowledge of plough building upon the Amorites.

Mercury (Roman)

Mercury, known for his swiftness, served as a messenger of the gods and was particularly associated with commerce and the grain trade. During late summer and early fall, he would travel from one place to another to remind people to bring in the harvest. The Gauls regarded him as a deity of agricultural abundance and commercial prosperity.

Osiris (Egyptian)

During times of famine in Egypt, the deity Neper, known for grains, gained popularity. Neper later became part of the cycle of life, death, and rebirth and was recognized as an aspect of Osiris. Osiris, like Isis, was associated with the harvest season. Donald MacKenzie details these stories in his book, "Egyptian Myths and Legend." Osiris was once a wise ruler who taught his people how to cultivate the land, sow seeds, and harvest crops. He also taught them how to grind corn and make flour and meal for sustenance and grow vine and fruit trees. Osiris was a leader who encouraged his people to worship the gods, build temples, and live virtuously, bringing Egypt peace and prosperity.

Parvati (Hindu)

Parvati is known as a consort of the god Shiva and is celebrated today as a goddess of harvest and protector of women during the annual Gauri Festival. While she is not mentioned in Vedic literature, her significance and influence are widely recognized.

Demeter (Greek)

In Greek mythology, the goddess Demeter is the equivalent of Ceres and is associated with seasonal changes. She is often linked to the Dark Mother image during late fall and early winter. When Hades abducted Demeter's daughter Persephone, her immense grief led to the earth's death for six months until Persephone's return.

Lugh (Celtic)

Lugh was recognized as a deity of proficiency and the equitable allocation of abilities. He is occasionally linked to midsummer due to his representation as a god of the harvest. During the summer solstice, the fields are thriving, ready to be gathered from the soil at Lughnasadh.

Pomona (Roman)

Pomona is known as the apple goddess, who is responsible for maintaining orchards and fruit trees. Unlike other agricultural deities, her focus is not on the harvest but on ensuring fruit trees' flourishing. Classical art often depicts her holding a tray of blossoming fruit or a cornucopia. Despite her obscurity, Pomona's likeness appears in numerous paintings by famous artists such as Rubens and Rembrandt and in sculptures.

Tammuz (Sumerian)

The deity worshipped by the Sumerians for harvest and vegetation is often linked to the cycle of life, death, and rebirth. According to Donald A. Mackenzie's book, Myths of Babylonia and Assyria: With Historical Narrative & Comparative Notes, Tammuz, the god mentioned in Sumerian hymns, is similar to Adonis. He lived on earth for a portion of the year as a shepherd and farmer, who was adored by the goddess Ishtar. He then passed away, allowing him to journey to the realm of Eresh-ki-gal (Persephone), the queen of Hades.

Neopaganism

In recent times, the belief system of Neopaganism has gained popularity. One of the major celebrations among Neopagans, particularly Celtic Neopagans, is Lughnasadh. The festival has diverse interpretations and can vary widely depending on the individual or group celebrating it.

Those following the traditional Lughnasadh festival strive to emulate historic celebrations as closely as possible. However, others incorporate various sources to create their unique celebrations.

Typically observed on 1 August in the Northern Hemisphere and 1 February in the Southern Hemisphere, Neopagan festivities usually commence at sunset on the previous evening. Some prefer to celebrate the midpoint between the summer solstice and autumn equinox or even during a full moon closest to this midpoint.

Celtic Reconstructionist

The Celtic Reconstructionist pagans are dedicated to preserving the ancient practices of the Celts through meticulous research and historical accounts. While they allow some modifications to adapt to modern life, they are committed to maintaining traditional Celtic forms and avoiding syncretic or eclectic approaches that blend different cultures.

For instance, faithful followers of Gaelic traditions celebrate Lughnasadh, the start of the harvest season, at a specific time - either when the "first fruits" appear or during the full moon closest in proximity. The designated fruit may vary depending on the region, such as blueberries in the Northeastern United States or blackberries in the Pacific Northwest. However, all recognize this period as an opportunity to express gratitude and offer sacrifices and supplications to their spiritual leaders.

During Lughnasadh, many bestow special honors upon Lugh himself, and any gentle rainfall is seen as a sign of his presence and blessings. Moreover, goddesses like Tailtiu are also fondly remembered during this crucial time, as they seek their assistance in ensuring the crops flourish without being disturbed by malevolent spirits known as Cailleachan, which could cause damage if left unchecked.

Wiccan

Many Wiccans honor Lammas or Lughnasadh as one of the eight festivals that comprise the Wheel of the Year. This celebration occurs during the first autumn harvest and falls between Midsummer and Mabon. Handfasting is considered a sacred practice during this time, along with Beltane. As a part of their observance, some Wiccans bake a figure of the "corn god" in bread, which is later symbolically sacrificed and consumed.

The Phases of the Moon

New

Sometimes called the Crescent Moon, when you can see the very first sliver of light in the sky. This phase promotes new beginnings, new endeavors and new relationships. It is the time to make positive changes and plant seeds of ideas that will be harvested later.

Waxing

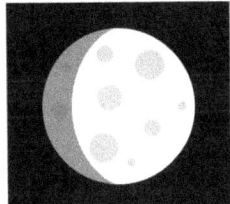

In this phase, the Moon appears to be growing in size, shifting from new to full as though it's gaining strength. It makes sense, then, that this is an excellent time to focus on increasing your knowledge, bank accounts and relationships. This phase promotes healing.

Full

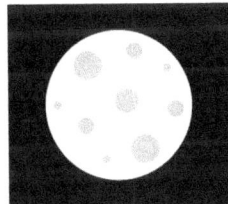

The Moon's most potent phase is when we see her entire illuminated face. This is a time of fulfillment, activity and increased psychic ability; for perfecting ideas, in other words, "getting your act together," celebrations or renewing commitments to people or projects—the best time for spells of any kind.

Waning

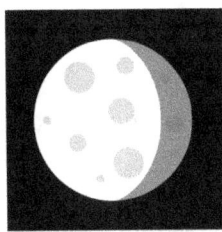

The Moon is decreasing in size as it journeys from full to dark. The waning Moon is a time of decrease, release, letting go and completion. An excellent time to begin dieting, breaking bad habits, breaking off relationships, or dealing with legal matters.

Oh Crap, a Full Moon!

Does the Moon influence our behavior or emotions? There's never been solid proof, but some new evidence suggests that the Moon can affect sleep, and it doesn't matter whether you're in the country or the city!

The Luna-Lunacy Connection

Ancient authorities like Aristotle, Paracelsus, and Pliny the Elder thought some humans were driven crazy by the full Moon. The Latin name for the Moon, "luna," is the root of modern words like "lunacy," "lunatic," and even "loon." (as in crazy as a loon).

Even today, many doctors, nurses, EMTs, police officers, and elementary school teachers agree that full Moons will bring out bizarre behavior; 43 percent of healthcare professionals believe in what some call "the lunar influence," as do 81 percent of mental healthcare specialists. But is there a lunar connection to abnormal behavior?

Unless you plan to ask a werewolf (which we don't recommend), it might be time to separate facts from fiction.

The Moon and Sleep

According to one scientific study conducted in 2021, people go to bed later and sleep for a shorter period in the days leading up to a full Moon. Specifically, people would go to bed 30 minutes later than average and sleep almost an hour less per night.

This makes sense because the light from the Moon after sunset is brighter on the days leading up to a full Moon. However, here's the surprising part: Studies found that it didn't matter if you lived in a rural or urban environment (where you might find more light pollution). So if the Moon's brightness isn't a factor, why do we stay up later and sleep less? One theory refers to our ancestors and our long history before the industrial age. People paid attention to the Moon and relied on its "night light" for hunting, fishing, and other social activities. Think of the "Harvest Moon" in the autumn, so named because it provided several nights of light for farmers to gather their crops at the height of harvest. Every month, the nights leading up to a full Moon bring more light to the evening.

Our natural circadian rhythms control our sleeping patterns; the day and night cycles are driven by Earth orbiting the Sun. But there are also circalunar rhythms, which are tied to lunar cycles. Indeed, some animals will respond to both circadian and lunar rhythms. Many animal species' behaviors are influenced by the Moon, too. For example, think of birds that rely on the Moon for migration and will even time their reproduction to coincide with the lunar cycle phases. Anecdotally, you have to wonder if less sleep (whether interrupted sleep or going to bed later) for several nights in a row might lead to some crankiness and what you might call moodiness. No, really!

The Moon and Lunacy

That leads us to weird behavior. There have been hundreds of studies about the Moon and lunacy. The few studies that suggest a connection are usually disproved or contradicted by others:

One study says more animal bites (from cats, rats, dogs, and horses) occur at the full Moon; another says there's no increase in dog bites.

One shows an increase in crime around the full Moon; others find no increase in arrests, calls for police assistance, prison assaults, batteries, or homicides.

Admissions for psychosis are lowest during the Full Moon, and psychiatric emergency room visits decline: but calls to suicide prevention hotlines peak at the new Moon, not the full Moon.

We're unsure how you'd prove the connection between the Moon and lunacy. But one explanation might be what psychologists call "confirmation bias." In other words, people are more likely to notice things that confirm a preexisting belief.

If you're working in an emergency room and something weird happens on the full Moon, your older and wiser colleagues nod and say: "Must be a full Moon." They likely heard from their elders when they were new at the job (Psychologists have a name for that, too: "communal reinforcement.").
But if something weird happens at a different lunar cycle phase, nobody says, "Must be the third quarter Moon!" And when nothing unusual happens on the full Moon, nobody says anything.

We call widespread beliefs that are unsupported by fact "folklore." Erika Brady, who teaches folklore at Western Kentucky University, says: "It's a way of imposing order on something that feels frighteningly out of control."

How does a belief that strange things happen on the full Moon help us feel safer? First, the full Moon occurs only once every 29.5 days; that means the other four weeks of the lunar month should be less dangerous and unpredictable.

Therefore, this folk belief implies that our fears about everything from increased bleeding to werewolves may be limited to only 12 or 13 days per year. (Maybe that's why the number 13 worries people!).

What do you think about the Moon? Does it influence behavior or emotions? Or, is it all in our imagination—and our dreams?

Moons of the Year

A rare second Full Moon in a single month is called a "Blue Moon." A rare second New Moon in a month is called a "Black Moon."

Different cultures gave the Moon different titles to express what the Moon means to them in a given month. As a result, some of the moon names make sense, while others may not make any sense.

Full Moon – January
Native American Tribes: Old Moon, Wolf Moon, Ice Moon, Moon after Yule, and Winter Moon
Siouan (Assiniboines) Tribe: Hard Time Moon
Inuit People of Northern Canada: Dwarf Seal Moon
Celtic: Wolf Moon, Stay Home Moon, Moon after Yule
Chinese: Holiday Moon
Fairy: Icicle Moon

Full Moon – February
Native American Tribes: Hunger or Starvation Moon, Storm Moon, Trapper's Moon, Moon of Ice, and Tree Moon
Siouan (Assiniboines) Tribe: Long Day Moon
Inuit People of Northern Canada: Seal Pup Moon
Celtic: Storm Moon, Ice Moon, and Snow moon
Chinese: Budding Moon
Fairy: Snowdrop Moon

Full Moon – March
Native American Tribes: Worm Moon, Crow Moon, Moon of Winds, Sap Moon, Fish Moon, Chaste Moon, and Death Moon
Siouan (Assiniboines) Tribe: Sore Eye Moon
Inuit People of Northern Canada: Snow Bird Moon
Celtic: Plough Moon, Wind Moon, Lenten (lengthening) Moon
Chinese: Sleeping Moon
Fairy: Waking Wood Moon

Moons of the Year

Full Moon – April
Native American Tribes: Pink Moon, Seed Moon, Frog Moon, Egg Moon, and Awakening Moon
Siouan (Assiniboines) Tribe: Frog's Moon
Inuit People of Northern Canada: Snow Melt Moon
Celtic: Budding Moon, New Shoots Moon, and Seed Moon
Chinese: Peony Moon
Fairy: Birthing Moon

Full Moon – May
Native American Tribes: Flower Moon, Hare Moon, Milk Moon, and Grass Moon
Siouan (Assiniboines) Tribe: Idle Moon
Inuit People of Northern Canada: Goose Moon
Celtic: Mother's Moon and Bright Moon
Chinese: Dragon Moon
Fairy: Moon of White Petals

Full Moon – June
Native American Tribes: Strawberry Moon, Planting Moon, and Green Corn Moon
Siouan (Assiniboines) Tribe: Full Leaf Moon
Inuit People of Northern Canada: Hunting Moon
Celtic: Mead Moon, Horse Moon, Dyan Moon, and Rose Moon
Chinese: Lotus Moon
Fairy: Wild Cherry Moon

Full Moon – July
Native American Tribes: Hay Moon, Summer Moon, Thunder Moon, and Buck Moon
Siouan (Assiniboines) Tribe: Red Berries Moon
Inuit People of Northern Canada: Dry Moon
Celtic: Claiming Moon, Wyrt or Herb Moon, and Mead Moon
Chinese: Hungry Ghost Moon
Fairy: Dancing Delight Moon

Full Moon – August
Native American Tribes: Sturgeon Moon, Corn Moon, Green Corn Moon, Dog Days Moon, and Lightening Moon
Siouan (Assiniboines) Tribe: Black Cherries Moon
Inuit People of Northern Canada: Swan Flight Moon
Celtic: Dispute Moon, Lynx Moon, and Grain Moon
Chinese: Harvest Moon
Fairy: Blackberry Harvest Moon

Moons of the Year

Full Moon – September
Native American Tribes: Singing Moon and Barley Moon
Siouan (Assiniboines) Tribe: Yellow Leaf Moon
Inuit People of Northern Canada: Harpoon Moon
Celtic: Wine Moon, Song Moon, Harvest Moon, and Barley Moon
Chinese: Chrysanthemum Moon
Fairy: Chestnut Moon

Full Moon – October
Native American Tribes: Traveller's Moon and Blackberry Moon
Siouan (Assiniboines) Tribe: Gophur Looks Back Moon
Inuit People of Northern Canada: Ice Moon
Celtic: Hunter's Moon, Blood Moon, and Seed Fall Moon
Chinese: Kindly Moon
Fairy: Moon of the Wild Hunt

Full Moon - November
Native American Tribes: Frosty Moon, Beaver Moon, Dark Moon, Tree Moon, Snow Moon, Freezing Moon, Ice Moon, and Migrating Moon
Siouan (Assiniboines) Tribe: Frost Moon
Inuit People of Northern Canada: Freezing Mist Moon
Celtic: Mourning Moon and Darkest Depths Moon
Chinese: White Moon
Fairy: Moon of the Wild Hunt

Full Moon – December
Native American Tribes: Cold Moon, Long Night Moon,
Siouan (Assiniboines) Tribe: Younger Hard Time Moon
Inuit People of Northern Canada: Dark Night Moon
Celtic: Oak Moon, Full Cold Moon
Chinese: Bitter Moon
Fairy: Mistletoe Moon

Days of the Week for Spells and Rituals

Monday
Best for psychic endeavors, invoking power, creative ideas, divine/inspirational messages, and healing.

Tuesday
Best for protection and building the strength of mind, body, and confidence.

Wednesday
Best for career/job issues, intellectual pursuits, travel
planning and research.

Thursday
Best for finances, legal matters, spirituality, and development.

Friday
Best for romantic attraction, all relationships, reconciliation, physical makeovers, and beautifying your environment.

Saturday
Best for home-related issues, brainstorming future projects, committing to personal goals, weight loss, releasing bad habits, ending relationships, etc.

Sunday
Best for healing (body, mind, soul), management/decision-making, insights into problem-solving, divine intervention/miracles, and unique friendships.

Do what makes you comfortable waiting for the "right" day to perform rituals or divination is unnecessary. So you do you, Boo!

Monday

Zodiac: Cancer
Solar System: Moon
Rune: Lagu
Numbers: 2, 9
Colors: Blue (pale), Gray, Silver, White
Tarot: High Priestess, Moon
Trees: Birch, Elder, Myrtle, Willow
Misc. Plants: Moonwort, Wormwood
Herb & Garden: Bluebell, Chamomile, Gardenia, Jasmine, Poppy, Rose (white), Violet
Gemstones & Minerals: Emerald, Moonstone, Quartz (clear, white), Sapphire
Metal: Silver
From the Sea: Pearl
Goddesses: Hecate, Selene
Gods: Aegir, Thoth
Angel or Magical Beings: Gabriel
Issues, Intentions & Powers: astral realm, clairvoyance, creativity, dream work, emotions, family, fertility, healing, the home, illumination, inspiration, intuition, love, magic (general, moon), prophecy, protection, psychic ability, travel, truth

Tuesday

Zodiac: Aries, Scorpio
Solar System: Mars
Rune: Tyr
Number: 5
Colors: Black, Orange, Red, Scarlet
Tarot: Strength, Wands (5, 6)
Trees: Cedar, Elm, Holly, Palm (dragon's blood)
Misc. Plants: Allspice, Ginger, Patchouli, Thistle
Herb & Garden: Basil, Garlic, Snapdragon
Gemstones & Minerals: Bloodstone, Emerald, Garnet, Ruby, Sapphire (star), Topaz
Metal: Iron
From the Sea:
Goddess:
God: Mars
Angel or Magical Beings: Elves
Issues, Intentions & Powers: action, aggression, assertiveness, battle/war, challenges, courage, discipline, energy, healing, honor, integrity, justice, passion, purification, strength, truth

Wednesday

Zodiac: Gemini
Solar System: Mercury
Rune: Odal
Number: 3
Colors: Orange, Purple, Silver, Violet, Yellow
Tarot: The Magician, Wheel of Fortune, Pentacles (8)
Trees: Aspen, Hazel, Rowan
Misc. Plant: Fern
Herb er Garden: Dill, Jasmine, Lavender, Lily of the Valley
Gemstones & Minerals: Agate, Amethyst, Aventurine, Lodestone, Opal, Ruby (star), Turquoise
Metal: Mercury
From the Sea:
Goddess: Athena
Gods: Hermes, Mercury, Odin
Angel or Magical Beings: Raphael
Issues, Intentions & Powers: business, cleverness, communication, creativity, crossroads, divination, fear, improvement (self), insight, intelligence, introspection, knowledge, loss, money, problems, skills, travel, wisdom

Thursday

Zodiac: Capricorn, Pisces
Solar System: Jupiter
Rune: Thorn
Numbers: 4, 8
Colors: Blue (royal), Green, Indigo, Purple
Tarot: Pentacles (ace, 9, 10)
Trees: Laurel, Maple, Oak, Pine
Misc. Plants: Cinnamon, Cinquefoil, Grain (wheat), Nutmeg
Herb & Garden: Honeysuckle, Sage
Gems & Minerals: Amethyst, Carnelian, Cat's Eye, Chrysoberyl, Sapphire, Turquoise
Metal: Tin
From the Sea:
Goddess: Juno
Gods: Jupiter, Thor, Zeus
Angel or Magical Beings:
Issues, Intentions & Powers: abundance, business, desire, endurance, fidelity, honor, justice (legal matters), leadership, loyalty, luck, money, prosperity, relationships, success, well-being

Friday

Zodiac: Taurus
Solar System: Venus
Rune: Peorth
Numbers: 6, 9
Colors: Aqua, Blue, Green, Indigo, Pink
Tarot: Empress, Lovers, Cups (2)
Trees: Apple, Birch, Myrtle
Misc. Plants: Saffron, Sandalwood
Herb & Garden: Feverfew, Raspberry, Rose, Strawberry, Thyme, Violet
Gemstones & Minerals: Alexandrite, Amber, Cat's Eye, Chrysoberyl, Emerald, Rose Quartz, Ruby
Metal: Copper
From the Sea:
Goddesses: Aphrodite, Freya, Frigg, Lakshmi, Venus
God: Eros
Angel or Magical Beings: Auriel
Issues, Intentions & Powers: beauty, emotions, fertility, friend/ ship, happiness, love, magic, passion, pleasure, romance, sex/uality, wisdom

Saturday

Zodiac: Aquarius
Solar System: Saturn
Rune: Dag
Number: 7
Colors: Black, Gray (dark), Indigo, Purple (dark)
Tarot: Temperance, Swords (knight, 2)
Trees: Alder, Cypress, Hawthorn, Pomegranate
Misc. Plants: Mullein, Myrrh
Herb & Garden: Morning Glory, Thyme
Gems & Minerals: Amethyst, Apache Tears, Diamond, Hematite, Jet, Labradorite, Turquoise
From the Sea:
Goddess: Hecate
God: Saturn
Angel or Magical Beings: Fairies
Issues, Intentions & Powers: banish, bind, business, death, discipline (self), freedom, justice, karma, life, limitations/ boundaries, money, motivation, negativity, obstacles, peace, problems, protection, willpower, wisdom

Sunday

Zodiac: Leo
Solar System: Sun
Rune: Sigel
Number: 1
Colors: Gold, Gray, Orange, Pink, White, Yellow
Tarot: Chariot, Sun, Wands (ace)
Trees: Ash, Birch, Laurel
Misc. Plants: Cinnamon, Frankincense
Herb & Garden: Carnation, Marigold, St. John's Wort, Sunflower
Gemstones & Minerals: Amber, Carnelian, Diamond, Quartz (clear), Sunstone, Tiger's Eye, Topaz
Metal: Gold
From the Sea: Pearl
Goddess: Brigid
God: Helios
Angel or Magical Beings: Elves
Issues, Intentions & Powers: accomplishment, action, ambition, attraction, authority, beauty, confidence, creativity, energy (solar), fame, freedom, friend/ship, goals, growth (personal), healing, hope, illumination, justice, leadership, light, money power (personal), pride, prosperity, protection, spirituality, strength, success, visions, warmth, well-being

Time of the Day for Spells and Rituals

Dawn

At dawn, the sun's fragile rays spread like a blanket of hope over an awakening world. At this time, choices are made, and paths unfold before us, full of life-giving potentiality.

Midday/Noon

Midday is when sunlight shines the strongest - a reminder of our strength and courage to tackle whatever lies ahead. It provides the motivation we need to persevere, no matter what obstacle stands in our way.

Dusk/Twilight

As dusk approaches, the sun bids a wistful farewell to the sky. Its goodbye is made of change and final goodbyes, an invitation to new beginnings if we're brave enough to open our hearts.

Midnight

At midnight, we come to the precipice of a journey into uncertainty; here is where paths diverge, and endings have no choice but to be accepted. It's an inevitable transition from one day to another, filled with promise yet also cloaked in sadness.

Do what makes you feel comfortable. There's no need to wait for the "right" time to perform rituals or divination. You do you, Boo!

Dawn

Zodiac:
Solar System: Venus
Runes: Beorc, Hagal, Thorn
Number:
Color:
Tarot: Swords
Trees:
Misc. Plants:
Herb & Garden:
Gemstones & Minerals:
Metal:
From the Sea:
Goddess: Brigid
Gods: Byelobog, Janus, Njord, Surya
Angel or Magical Beings: Raphael
Issues, Intentions & Powers: activate/awaken, beginnings, crossroads, fertility, hope, life (vitality), light, nurture, purpose, romance, youth

Midday/Noon

Zodiac: Leo
Solar System: Sun
Runes: Dag, Rad, Sigel
Number:
Color:
Tarot: Wands
Trees:
Misc. Plants:
Herb & Garden:
Gemstones & Minerals:
Metal:
From the Sea:
Goddess:
God: Byelobog
Angel or Magical Beings: Michael
Issues, Intentions & Powers: determination, obstacles, strength, willpower

Dusk/Twilight

Zodiac: Cancer
Solar System: Venus
Runes: Feoh, Jer, Peorth
Numbers:
Colors:
Tarot: Cups
Trees:
Misc. Plants:
Herb & Garden:
Gemstones & Minerals:
Metal:
From the Sea:
Goddess:
God:
Angel or Magical Beings: Gabriel
Issues, Intentions & Powers: banish, change(s), endings, the otherworld/underworld, sorrow

Midnight

Zodiac: Taurus
Solar System: Earth, Venus
Runes: Is, Tyr, Ur
Number:
Color:
Tarot: Pentacles
Trees:
Misc. Plants:
Herb & Garden:
Gemstones & Minerals:
Metal:
From the Sea:
Goddess:
God:
Angel or Magical Beings: Auriel
Issues, Intentions & Powers: crossroads, endings, release

Astrological Signs

Aries
March 21 - April 19
for those born under the sign of
The Ram

Taurus
April 20 - May 20
for those born under the sign of
The Bull

Gemini
May 21 - June 20
for those born under the sign of
The Twins

Cancer
June 21 - July 22
for those born under the sign of
The Crab

Leo
July 23 - August 22
for those born under the sign of
The Lion

Virgo
August 23 - September 22
for those born under the sign of
The Virgin

Libra
September 23 - October 22
for those born under the sign of
The Scales

Scorpio
October 23 - November 21
for those born under the sign of
The Scorpion

Sagittarius
November 22 - December 21
for those born under the sign of
The Archer

Capricorn
December 22 - January 19
for those born under the sign of
The Goat

Aquarius
January 20 - February 18
for those born under the sign of
The Water Bearer

Pisces
February 19 - March 20
for those born under the sign of
The Fishes

Leo

July 23rd - August 22nd

Solar System: Sun
Runes: As, Rad, Wyn
Numbers: 1, 4, 5, 8
Colors: Gold, Green, Orange, Red, Scarlet, Yellow
Tarot: Strength, Sun, Wands
Trees: Acacia, Hazel, Holly, Juniper, Laurel, Oak, Olive, Palm, Walnut
Misc. Plants: Anise, Cinnamon, Clove, Eyebright, Frankincense, Mistletoe, Nutmeg, Saffron, Sandalwood
Herb & Garden: Angelica, Borage, Chamomile, Daffodil, Dill, Goldenseal, Heliotrope, Honeysuckle, Lavender, Marigold, Peony, Raspberry, Rosemary, Rue, St. John's Wort, Sunflower
Gemstones & Minerals: Amber, Beryl (golden), Carnelian, Chrysoberyl, Citrine, Danburite, Diamond, Garnet, Jasper, Kunzite, Labradorite, Larimar, Onyx, Peridot, Rhodochrosite, Ruby, Sapphire, Sardonyx, Sunstone, Tiger's Eye, Topaz, Zircon
Metal: Gold, Iron
From the Sea:
Goddesses: Anat, Bast, Cybele, Devi, Diana, Durga, Freya, Hathor, Hera, Inanna, Ishtar, Juno, Nanna, Sekhmet
Gods: Amun, Helios, Mithras, Nergal, Ra, Vishnu
Angel: Michael
Issues, Intentions & Powers: action, affection, ambition, authority, communication (eloquent), confidence, courage, creativity, determination, energy, enlightenment, enmity, friendship, generosity, growth, guardian, guidance, integrity, jealousy, leadership, life (zest), light, love, loyalty, magic (animal, sex), passion, pleasure, power, pride, romance, strength (controlled), warmth, willpower

Message:
This is the perfect time to take action. Trust your instincts, be courageous in your leadership, and show compassion in your commitment. Clearly express your goals and find a renewed sense of determination and excitement that could surprise you.

Virgo

August 23rd - September 22nd

Solar System: Earth and Mercury
Runes: Boerc and Ken
Numbers: 6, 9
Colors: Black, Blue (navy), Brown 9dark), Gold, Gray (dark), Green, Pink, Purple, Violet, White, and Yellow
Tarot: Hermit and Magician
Trees: Beech, Chestnut, Cypress, Hazel, Horse Chestnut, Maple, Mimosa, Oak, and Walnut
Misc. Plants: Eyebright, Horehound, Patchouli, Sandalwood, and Skullcap
Herb & Garden: Aster, Bergamot, Dill, Fennel, Honeysuckle, Hyacinth, Lavender, Lily, Lily of the Valley, Marjoram, Peppermint, Rosemary, Valerian, Violet
Gemstones & Minerals: Agate, Amazonite, Amethyst, Andalusite, Apatite, Aquamarine, Aventurine, Carnelian, Chrysocolla, Diamond, Emerald, Garnet, Jade, Jasper (pink), Lapis Lazuli, Lodestone, Moss Agate, Opal, Peridot, Sapphire, Sardonyx, Sugilite, Tourmaline (watermelon), Tsavorite, Turquoise, and Zircon (red)
Metal: Mercury
From the Sea:
Goddesses: Anat, Artemis, Demeter, Diana, Hestia, Inanna, Iris, Ishtar, Isis, Kore, Nanna, Persephone, and Vesta
God: Odin
Angel: Auriel
Issues, Intentions & Powers: abundance, beginnings, consciousness, cycles, destiny, emotions, endings, grounding, independence, intuition, love, the mind (analytical), nurture, order/organize, purification, sexuality, shyness, success (business), and well-being

Message:
It's important to maintain balance and stability by staying grounded. While creativity can lead to financial success, it's important to remain humble. Don't shy away from unexpected events and prioritize self-care by taking nature walks, practicing meditation, and engaging in positive social interactions. Wishing you a transformative time ahead.

Libra

September 23rd - October 22nd

Solar System: Saturn and Venus
Runes: Hagal, Tyr, and Wyn
Numbers: 7
Colors: Black, Blue (light), Royal Blue, Brown, Green, Lavender, Pink, Violet, and Yellow
Tarot: Empress and Justice
Trees: Apple, Aspen, Cherry, Hazel, Magnolia, Maple, and Witch Hazel
Misc. Plants: Aloe, Belladonna, Burdock, Mullein, and Vanilla
Herb & Garden: Catnip, Dandelion, Foxglove, Lilac, Marjoram, Mugwort, Passion Flower, Pennyroyal, Rose, Spearmint, Strawberry, Thyme, and Violet
Gemstones & Minerals: Agate, Ametrine, Aquamarine, Beryl, Bloodstone, Chrysoprase, Citrine, Desert Rose, Diamond, Emerald, Iolite, Jade, Jasper, Kunzite, Kyanite, Lapis Lazuli, Lepidolite, Malachite, Moonstone, Opal, Rose Quartz, Sapphire, Smoky Quartz, Sunstone, Tourlimine (black, blue, and pink), and Zircon (red)
Metal: Copper
From the Sea: Coral (red)
Goddesses: Aphrodite, Athena, Frigg, Isis, Justitia, Maat, Minerva, Nemesis, and Venus
God: Cernunnos, Hephaestus, Mithras, Njord, Shiva, Thoth, and Vishnu
Angel: Raphael
Issues, Intentions & Powers: attraction, balance, beauty, business, community, cooperation, fairness, grace, harmony, justice, love, marriage, relationships, romance, sensitivity, sensuality, sympathy, and unity

Message:
Achieving balance in all areas of life, be it work or leisure, is crucial. Keep yourself receptive to building deep emotional connections in your relationships and make efforts to nurture them.

Magic of the Months

January - beginnings, healing, money protection, and strength
February - astral realm, banish, beginnings, empowerment, fertility, and purification
March - fertility, innocence, prosperity, spirituality, and success
April - beginnings, fertility, growth, and spirituality
May - divination, enchantment, fertility, love, and well being
June - abundance, love, marriage, prosperity, and relationships
July - dream work, light, magic, purpose, and strength
August - abundance, magic (animal), prophecy, prosperity, and wisdom
September - confidence, the home, manifestation, and protection
October - courage, healing, inspiration, memory/memories, and stability
November - cooperation, darkness, divination, healing, and hope
December - dedication/devotion, love, peace, prosperity, and strength

Colors of the Month

January - gray, purple, and white
February - black, blue, and red
March - green and white
April - brown and green
May - pink
June - purple and red
July - green and yellow
August - green (dark) and yellow
September - brown
October - black and blue
November - blue (pale), green, and silver
December - black and red

Crystals of the Months

January - garnet (rhodolite), moonstone, rose quartz, ruby, tourmaline (red)
February - amethyst, moonstone, obsidian, onyx, topaz, zircon (red)
March - aquamarine, bloodstone, jasper, opal, topaz (blue)
April - beryl, diamond, malachite, sapphire, and zircon
May - agat, carnelian, emerald, garnet, rose quartz, tourmaline, and tsavorite
June - agate, alexandrite, cat's eye, chrysoberyl, emerald, garnet, moonstone, and ruby
July - carnelian, malachite, onyx, ruby, sapphire, spinel, tourmaline (red), and turquoise
August - carnelian, emerald, jade, moonstone, peridot, sardonyx, topaz, and tourmaline
September - carnelian, cat's eye, iolite, lapis lazuli, peridot, sapphire, and spinel (blue)
October - aquamarine, garnet, kunzite, morganite, opal, sapphire, and tourmaline
November - beryl, cat's eye, chrysoberyl, citrine, sapphire (yellow), and topaz
December - aquamarine, bloodstone, ruby, topaz (blue), turquoise, and zircon

Tarot Cards

Tarot is an intricate divination system consisting of 78 cards divided into major and minor arcana cards. Heavily relying on classical mythology and symbolism, tarot allows one to receive answers to events by interpreting messages based on how the cards are dealt. This can be done utilizing card spreads like the classic Celtic cross or a simple 3 card past, present, and future layout.

Oracle Cards

Less structured than tarot, oracle cards use a combination of artwork and written interpretations, which can sometimes include exercises. Oracle cards can be based on nearly any subject matter and are open to various styles and formats. Perfect for guiding without the intricacies associated with tarot.

Draw Your Cards

There are multiple ways to select the cards for your reading.
Cutting the deck with one hand and pulling the card on top is a simple, no-nonsense approach. Another way is to hold the deck in one hand and tilt it to reveal a gap; you can take the top card. Next, you can fan the cards out and choose the card your intuition pulls you to. Finally, draw a single card for a simple reading or several cards for what's known as a spread. Tarot spreads can speak more broadly to your situation. The more cards you use in a spread, the more in-depth the reading tends to be, but a big spread can be overwhelming for beginners.

After you choose your card(s), lay them down in your pattern for the spread. Now you can gaze at them, pay attention to what comes immediately to mind, and then go from there.

Interpret the card(s) you draw.
Stay focused on the cards and the feelings you get, connect the cards to your senses and write down what comes to mind. After your impressions are completely logged, look in the companion book for the general meaning of the cards you pulled. That's it. Eazy Peezey.

Lughnasadh

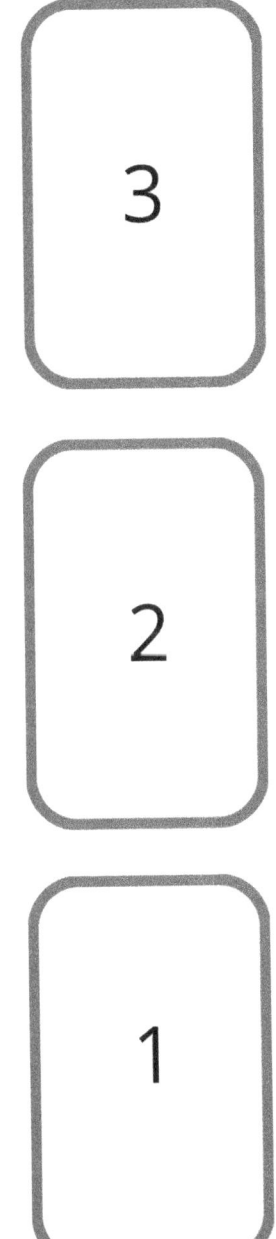

Lughnasadh

Card 1 - What I need to let go of
Card 2 - Something I need to pay attention to
Card 3 - What to embrace for full growth

Impressions:

Leo

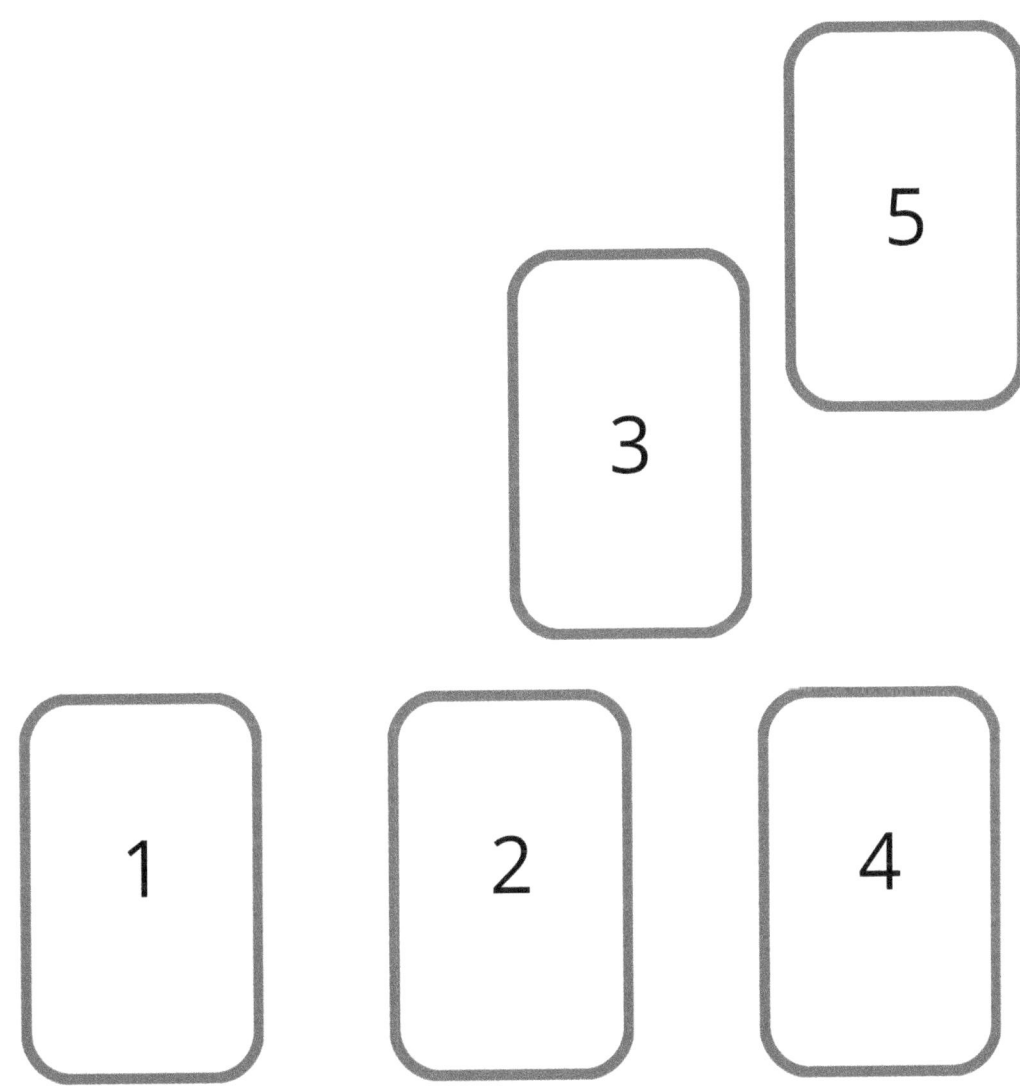

Leo

Card 1 - How to brave this season
Card 2 - How to enjoy myself
Card 3 - How to be safely seen
Card 4 - What to burn away
Card 5 - Where to shine my light

Impressions:

Virgo

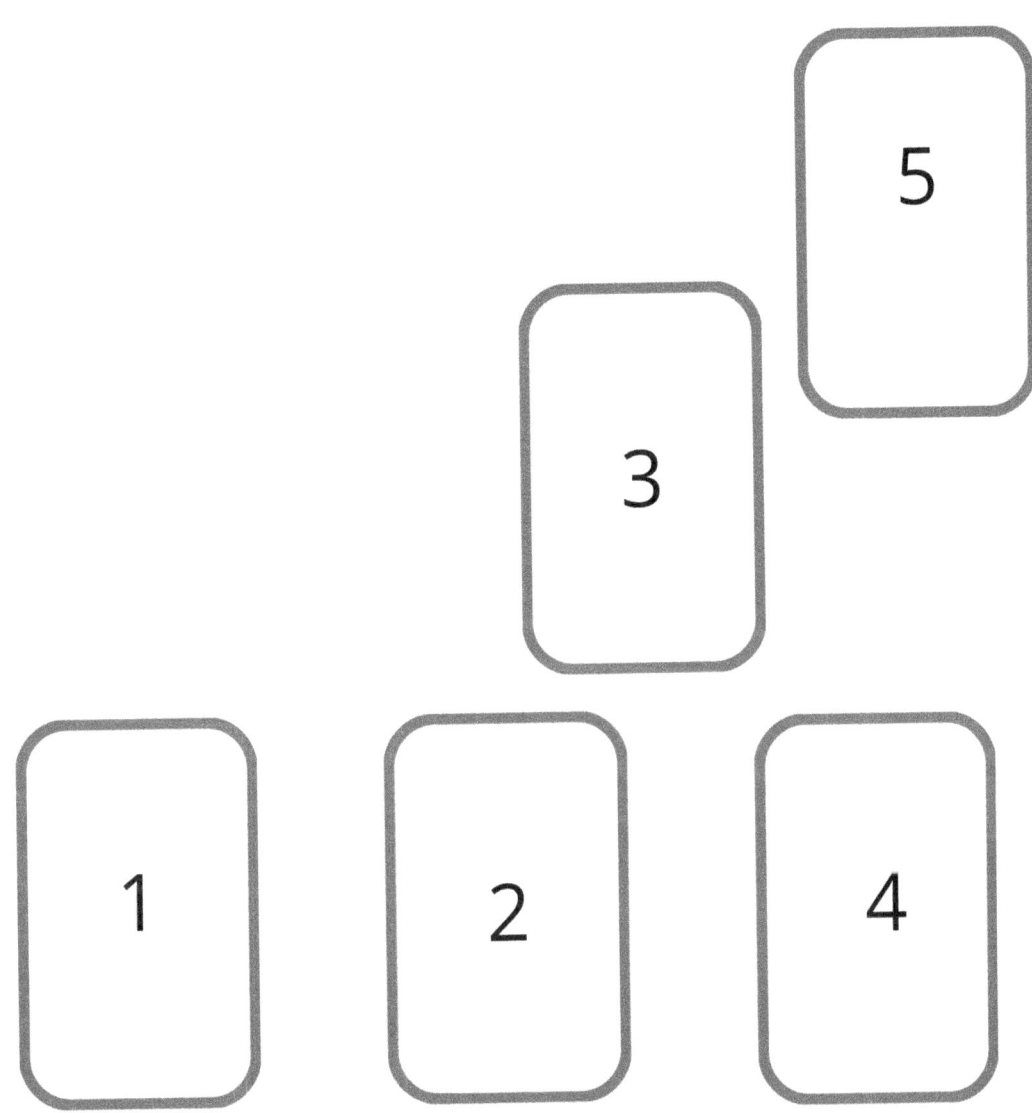

Virgo

Card 1 - How to bring me back down to Earth
Card 2 - What needs organizing
Card 3 - Details to focus on
Card 4 - How to reach my goals and get things done
Card 5 - How to surrender and trust

Impressions:

Needs

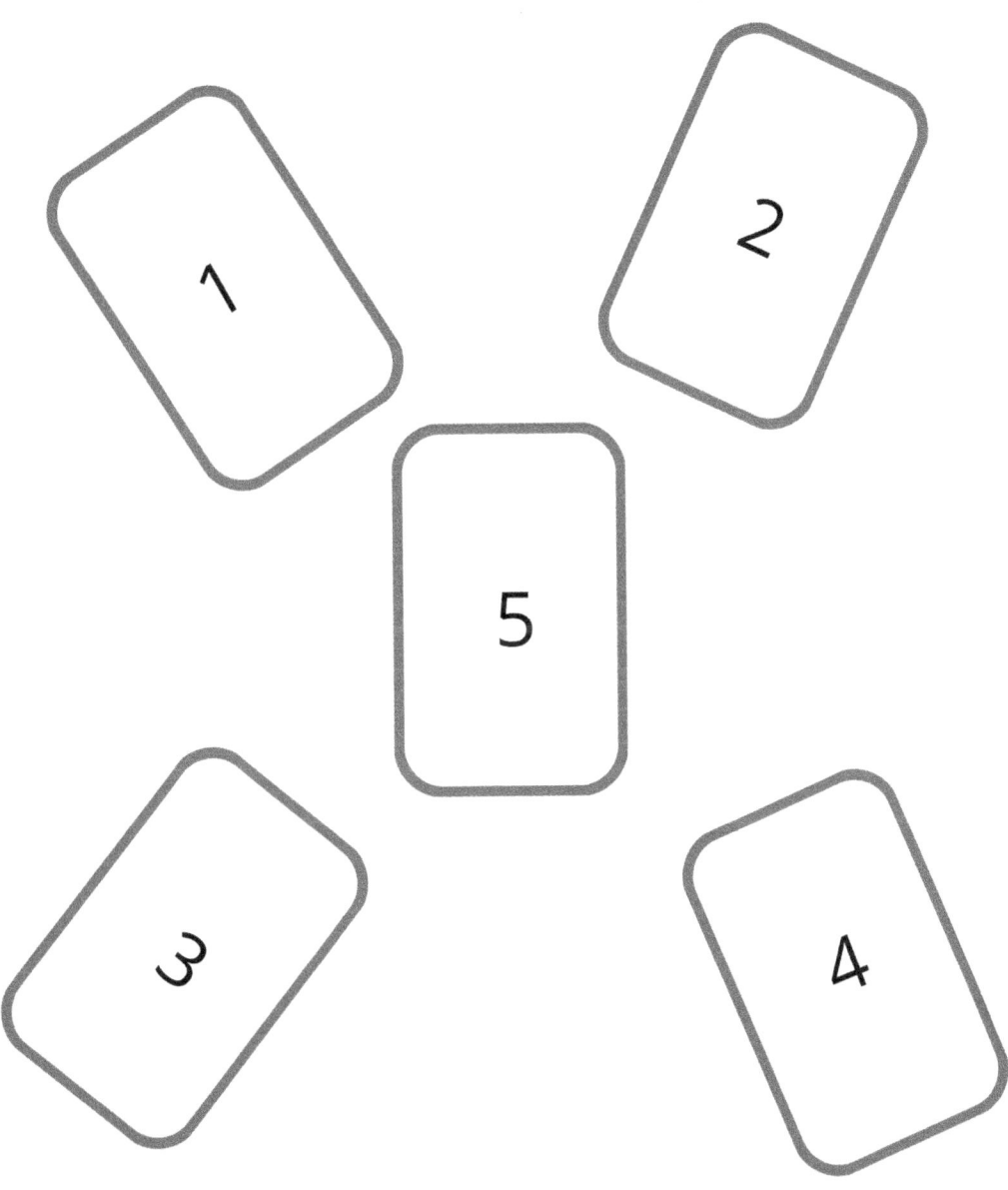

Needs

Card 1 - Physically, I need...
Card 2 - Emotionally, I need...
Card 3 - Mentally, I need...
Card 4 - Spiritually, I need...
Card 5 - How I currently feel

Impressions:

Growth

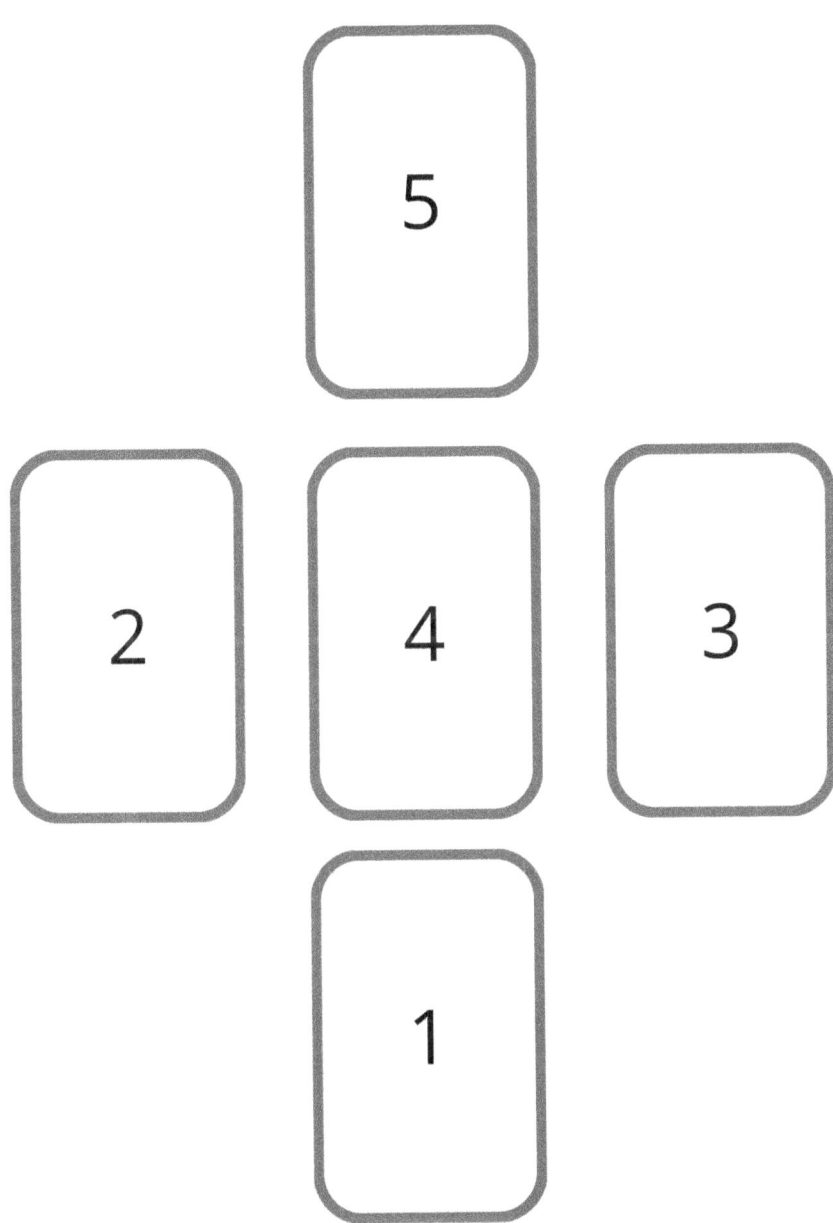

Growth

Card 1 - A part of myself that I am outgrowing
Card 2 - How I can shed this layer gracefully
Card 3 - Why this change is essential for me to
Card 4 - How this alters my life moving forward
Card 5 - A message from spirit

Impressions:

New Moon

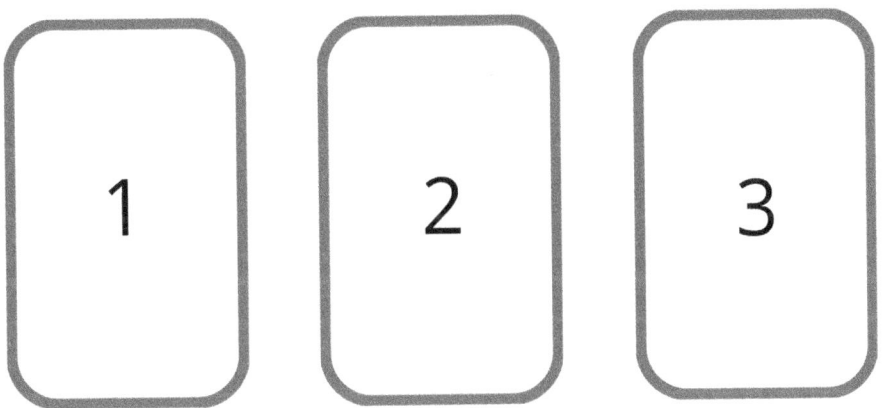

New Moon

Card 1 - What I need to focus on during the next lunar cycle
Card 2 - What do I need to let go
Card 3 - What is the next step I should consider

Impressions:

Full Moon

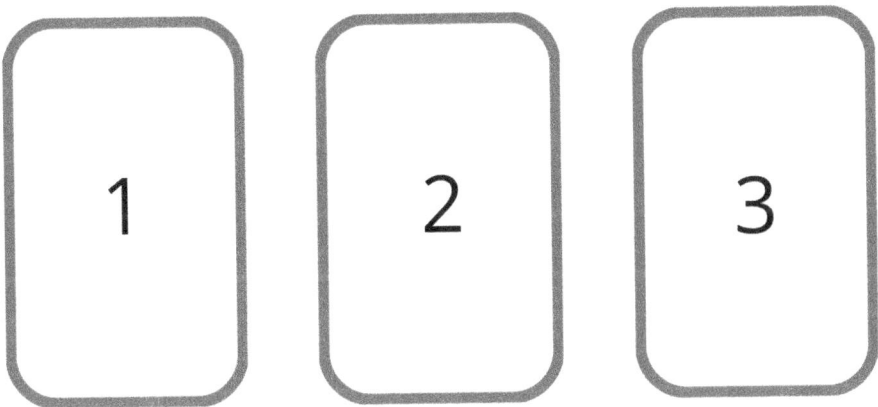

Full Moon

Card 1 - Where do I need to be mindful of excess
Card 2 - What has been building from the new moon to the full moon to be released
Card 3 - How can I engage fully in that release and ready myself for the next phase

Impressions:

Sun, Moon, Stars

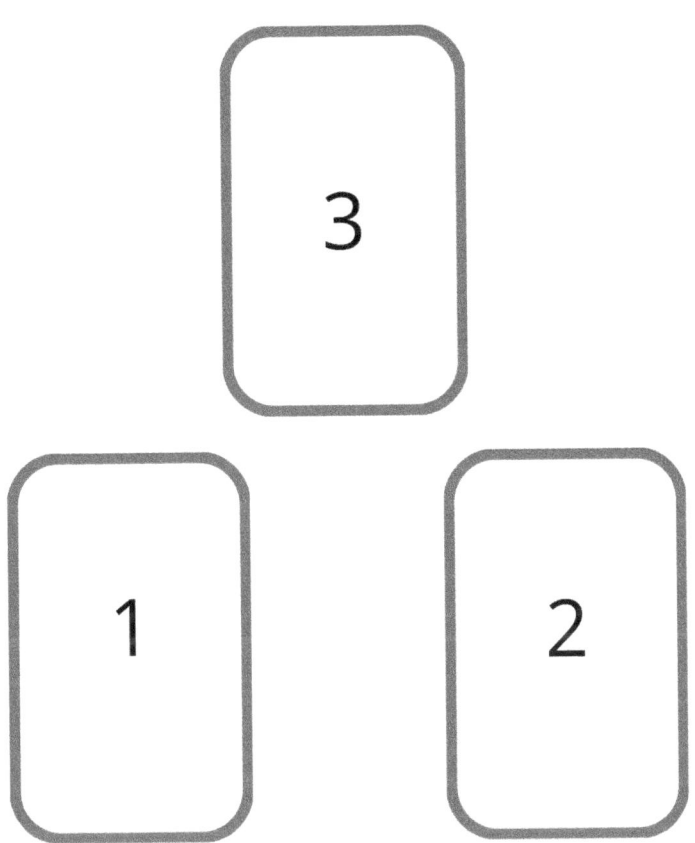

Sun, Moon, Stars

Card 1 - Sun: How others see you or project onto the world
Card 2 - Moon: A shadow aspect your subconscious is looking to assimilate
Card 3 - Stars: Your unique and possible untapped gift

Impressions:

Strength and Weakness

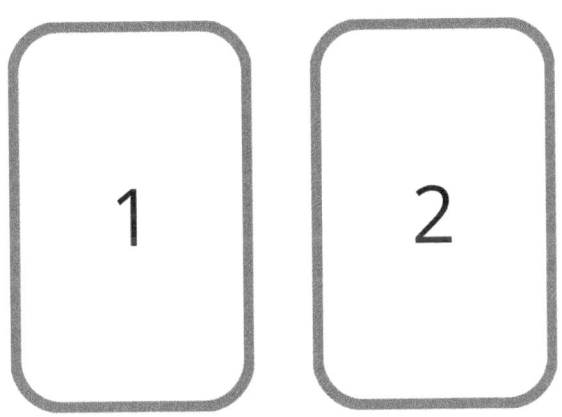

Strength and Weakness

Card 1 - What is my strength
Card 2 - What is my weakness

Impressions:

Blockage

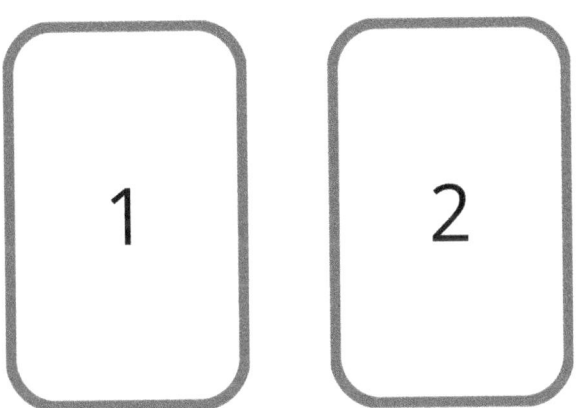

Blockage

Card 1 - What is my blockage
Card 2 - What is my solution

Impressions:

Shit Sucks

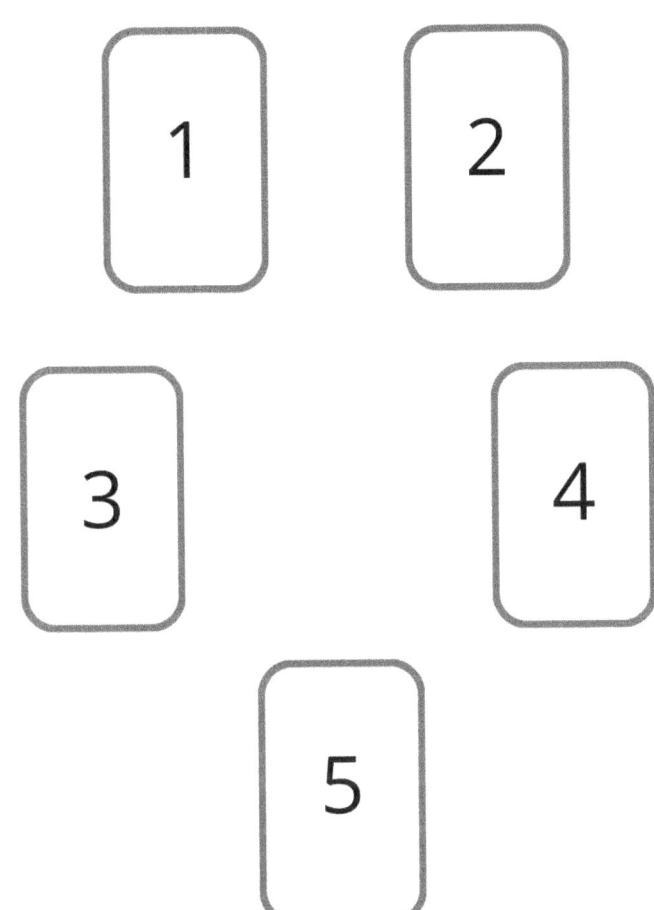

Shit Sucks

Card 1 - What can I change
Card 2 - How to do it
Card 3 - What don't I have power over (life lesson learned)
Card 4 - What aspects of myself are the life lesson changing
Card 5 - What will I have learned when the lesson is over
Impressions:

What Do I Really Want

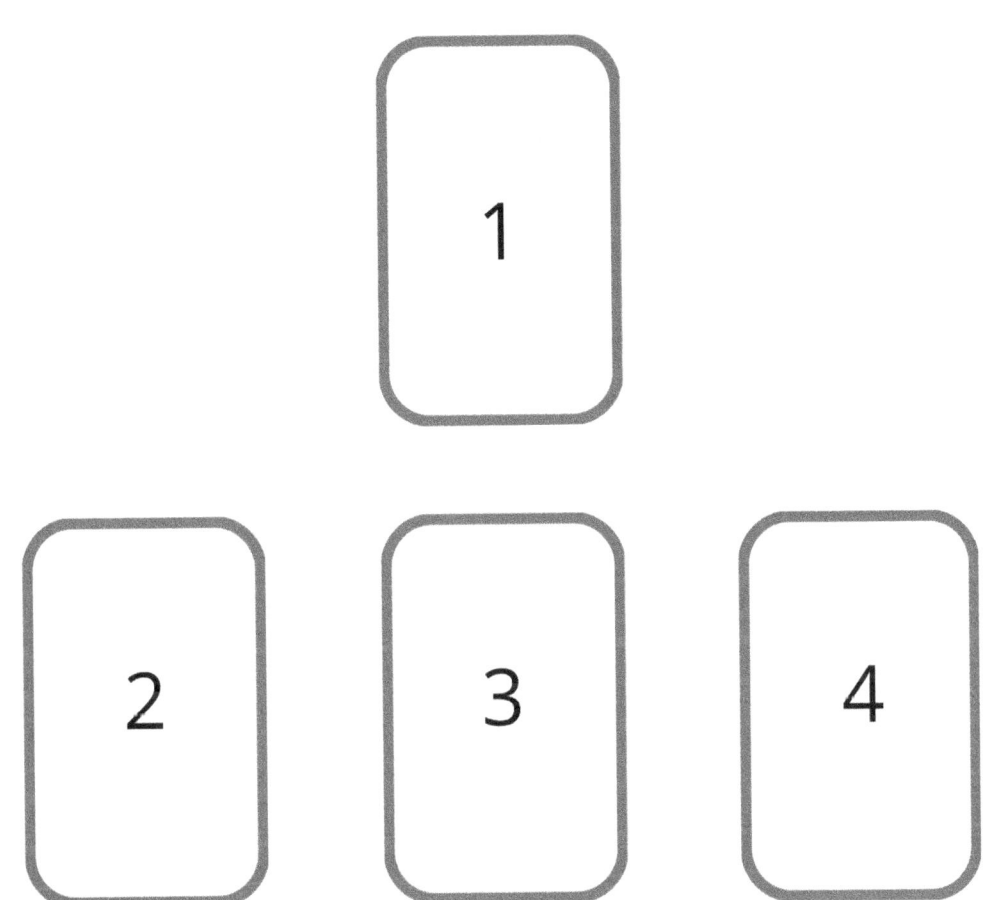

What Do I Really Want

Card 1 - You and the state of things
Card 2 - What you really want (desires, wishes, and dreams)
Card 3 - What you can do to make Card 2 happen
Card 4 - Outcome if you take step 3

Impressions:

Myself

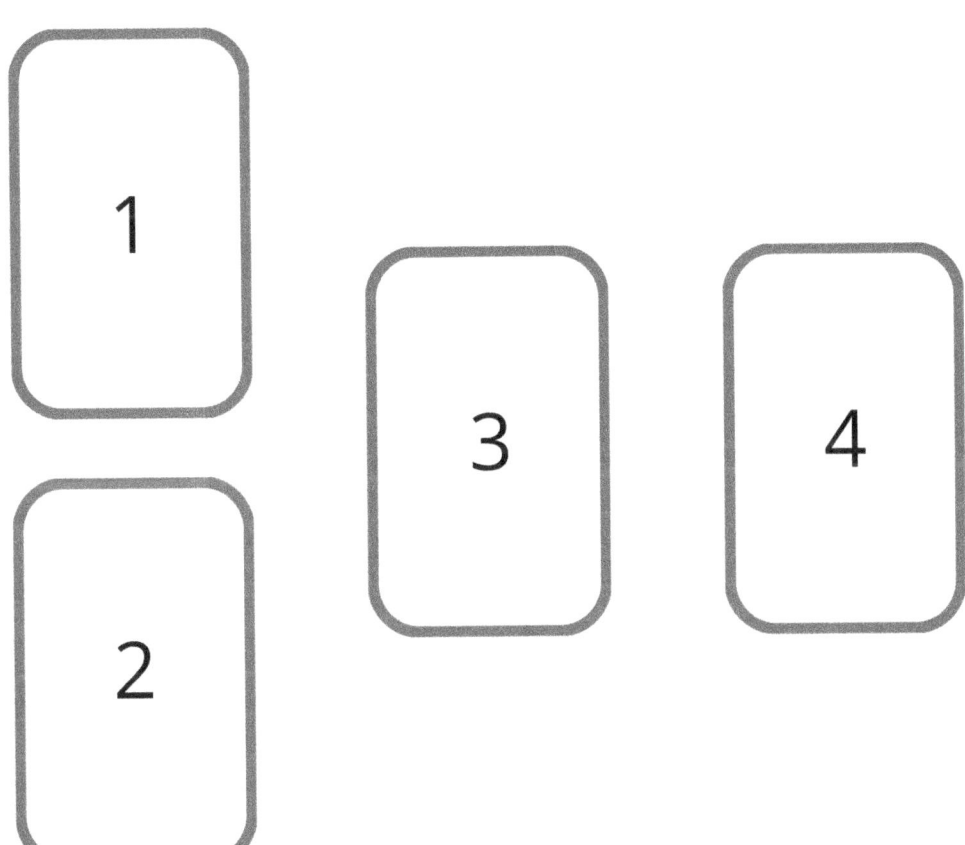

Myself

Card 1 - Am I fully using my time and tools to guide my goals
Card 2 - What message(s) have I been avoiding
Card 3 - How can I show myself love and self-care
Card 4 - Where is my attention needed most this summer

Impressions:

Colors at First Glance

Bringing balance to our lives with color energy is easy. We can do it by wearing our favorite colors, painting rooms in calming colors, or adding different colors to our decor. If we pay attention to the colors around us and how they make us feel, we can use them to improve our lives and increase our vibrations.

Black for banishing, protection, binding, releasing, and defense.

Green for money, prosperity, employment, fertility, growth, luck, abundance, and your Heart Chakra.

Red for strength, passion, courage, action, survival, love, and your Root Chakra.

Yellow for intellect, confidence, travel, movement, joy, imagination, productivity, willpower, and your Solar Plexus Chakra.

Orange for attraction, energy, legal matters, ambition, vitality, opportunity, creativity, inspiration, and your Sacral Chakra.

White for protection, purification, peace, purity, tranquility, and balance.

Blue for healing, peace, forgiveness, communication, truth, calming, focus, memory, and your Throat Chakra.

Purple for spirituality, wisdom, peace, harmony, intuition, psychic abilities, divination, dreams, and your Third Eye Chakra.

But remember to do what feels right to you.
As always: You Do You, Boo!

Candle Color Usage

Using color in spells and rituals can be a powerful way to enhance their energy. Color energy is easy to use and can be woven into your candles, spells, and rituals.

Black - banishing, binding, cord cutting, and endings

Green - money, luck, prosperity, and growth

Red - passion, sex, love, health, and courage

Yellow - intelligence, mental health, memory, and confidence

Orange - happiness, justice, creativity, and flexibility

White - serenity, healing, renewal, and cleansing

Blue - wisdom, dreams, calm, and communication

Purple - divination, intuition, spirituality, and transformation

Pink - empathy, kindness, romance, and generosity

Brown - happiness, justice, creativity, and flexibility

Gold - fortune, enlightenment, talents, and strength

Silver - dreams, moon energy, enchantment, and inspiration

Auras

Are in constant motion with every breath.

They are not always the same color.

Are a physical representation of the energy surrounding your physical body

May have one or more colors per layer.

Are not a perfectly rounded shape.

They are multidimensional (above, below, and all around you).

Are composed of layers that may blend into each other.

Surround every living thing (human, plant, animal).

Need regular cleansing.

Can rip and tear due to physical injury.

Need maintenance to repair rips, holes, and tears.

Can expand up to 30 feet outside your physical body.

Help you to feel external energies.

Are a natural part of your body.

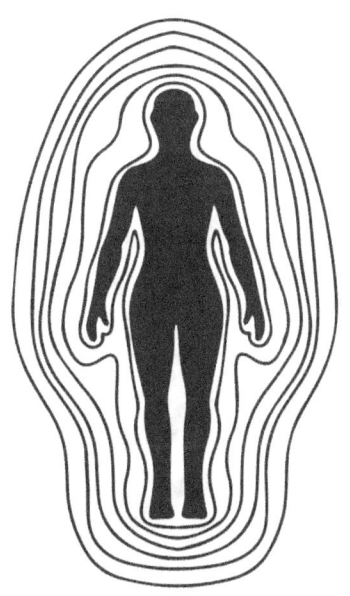

Aura Layers

Aura layers, starting on the outside and moving inward:

1 Ketheric Template
2 Celestial/Divine
3 Etheric Template
4 Astral
5 Mental
6 Emotional
7 Etheric

Aura Colors

Yellow
Energetic, optimistic, confident, childlike, fun-loving, sensitive, happy, free-spirited, creative, generous, and connects with nature and animals.

Orange
Creative, independent, adventurous, risk-taker, resourceful, strategic, loves to test physical limits, mentally focused, and overcomes challenges.

Blue
Loving, nurturing, compassionate, sensitive, forgiving, loyal, spiritual, emotional depth, teaching, caretaker of people and the planet.

Red
Intense, passionate, hard-working, grounded, literal, raw courage, sensual, honest, self-confident, experiences the world through touch.

Green
Healing, teaching, organized, entrepreneurial, highly intelligent, driven, successful, perfectionist, empowers others, ability to accomplish goals.

Magenta
Non-conformist, creative, intelligent, free-spirited, eccentric, original, likes to be the center of attention, strong-willed, unique, and innovative.

Tan
Detail-oriented, practical, cautious, private, calm, clean, logical, intuitive, committed, values love, gentle, analytical, controlled.

Violet
Artistic/creative, visionary, loves to take chances, enjoys travel, charismatic leader, humanitarian, inspirational to others, has big ideas.

Lavender
Enchanting, daydreamer, fragile, sensitive, imaginative, creative, intelligent, gentle, intuitive, love to change directions.

Indigo
Wise, intuitive, believe in higher ideals + principles, peaceful, creative, non-judgemental, spiritually gifted, sensitive, enlightened consciousness.

White
Gifted healer, highly spiritual, quiet, sensitive, one with nature, adaptable, highly intuitive, loves simplicity, meditative, calming.

At A Glance Chakras

Crown Chakra
Sahasrara
Represents spiritual consciousness and transformation.

Third Eye Chakra
Ajna
Responsible for spiritual communication, awareness, and perception.

Throat Chakra
Visuddha
Governs self-expression, communication, and the ability to speak one's truth.

Heart Chakra
Anahata
Governs people's love for themselves and those around them, supporting empathy, compassion, and forgiveness.

Solar Plexus Chakra
Manipura
Represents confidence, self-esteem, and personal power.

Sacral Chakra
Svadhisthana
It supports emotional and physical health aspects and governs many of the body's fluids (from the sex organs, the bladder, and the kidneys).

Root Chakra
Muladhara
Good health in the body, a sense of connection to the Earth, and a feeling of support and stability in the physical world.

Chakra Symbols

Crown Chakra:
To Know and Understand

Third Eye:
To See

Throat Chakra:
To Speak and Be Heard

Heart Chakra:
To Love and Be Loved

Solar Plexus Chakra:
To Act

Sacral Chakra:
To Feel and Desire

Root Chakra:
To Be Here and To Have

Chakras

Chakra is a Sanskrit word meaning wheel or vortex. They are an integral part of the body's energy system and transformers of subtle energy. They take the Ki around us and transform it into the various frequencies our subtle energy system needs to keep us healthy.

The Root Chakra (1st) — Reproductive glands (testes in men; ovaries in women); controls sexual development and secretes sex hormones. This chakra is located in the pelvic region at the base of the spine. It is responsible for our physical reality, safety, security, and survival instincts.

The Sacral Chakra (2nd) — Adrenal glands; regulates the immune system and metabolism. This chakra influences our emotions and creativity. It's located just a few inches below the belly button. In addition, this chakra affects our views on intimacy, boundaries, and trust.

The Solar Plexus Chakra (3rd) — Pancreas; regulates metabolism. This chakra is situated in the upper belly, at the diaphragm. It guides our will and mental layers. It is also responsible for our energy, personal power, and issues related to the Ego.

The Heart Chakra (4th) — Thymus gland; regulates the immune system.
The heart chakra is located in the center of the chest and governs our ability to experience unconditional love. This chakra also influences our relationships and how we demonstrate compassion and hope.

The Throat Chakra (5th) — Thyroid gland; regulates body temperature and metabolism. It governs our ability to communicate clearly and effectively. When this chakra is balanced, we can express ourselves truthfully and listen and understand others better.

The Third Eye Chakra (6th) — Pituitary gland; produces hormones and governs the function of the previous five glands; sometimes, the pineal gland is linked to the third eye chakra and the crown chakra. The third eye chakra is a powerful tool for intuition and spiritual insight. It is located behind the middle of the forehead, near the pineal gland. This chakra helps us to open up to greater awareness, psychic senses, and spiritual gifts.

The Crown Chakra (7th) — Pineal gland; regulates biological cycles, including sleep.
This chakra, located at the top of the head, is associated with spirituality and our connection to higher intelligence. It helps us to achieve enlightenment. By opening this chakra, we can access greater knowledge and guidance.

How to Use Chakra Affirmations

Meditation: You can connect with one or all of your chakras during a single meditation. For instance, if you're connecting with the root chakra, envision it as a bright red glowing orb at the base of your spine. As you breathe in, see the orb getting bigger. As you breathe out, see it growing brighter. As you do this, recite grounding root chakra affirmations. To connect with each of your chakras in a single meditation, start at the root chakra and repeat one or two affirmations. Then, move to the sacral chakra and work upwards along your spine.

Mirror Work: Stand in front of the mirror and look yourself in the eyes. Take a deep breath and focus on one chakra at a time. You can look at the physical location of the chakra in the mirror but also try to connect to it within. Recite the chakra affirmations that your soul needs most at this moment.

Post-Its: Leave post-it notes in visible places you'll see throughout the day. On each post-it note, write a chakra affirmation that resonates with you. Then, whenever you see the post-it note, recite the affirmation silently or out loud, feeling the positive words in every cell of your being. For a bonus, you can use post-its that correlate with the color of each chakra.

Color Therapy: Color therapy is the act of immersing yourself in the color associated with that chakra. One way to use color therapy and affirmations in conjunction is to make it a game. For instance, if you're working with your heart chakra, pay attention to the world around you as you go about your day. Then, recite a heart chakra affirmation silently or aloud whenever you see something green in your external world. You can do this with one or multiple chakras at a time.

Grounding

Grounding is a straightforward and natural way to connect ourselves back to Earth. We often hear people talking about grounding and telling us to ground ourselves, but why do we need to do it, and how do we do it?

Some of us are more prone than others to live in the clouds, so we do not feel deeply rooted in our bodies. If this happens occasionally, it is acceptable; however, if this becomes a permanent state of being, it can lead to some problems.

Ungrounded Symptoms:
High sensitivity to light and noise.
Not finding the keys or other things, constantly dropping stuff, forgetting appointments, etc.
Constantly daydreaming.
Feeling dizzy and spaced out.
Cannot meditate and constantly falling asleep during the exercise.
Feeling tired, drained, and lacking energy.
Feeling grumpy and nervy.
Losing track of what a person says to me, unable to converse normally.
Getting lost while driving/walking, even in familiar areas.
Unable to see synchronicities happening in our lives.
Feeling ungrounded can make life difficult, like sometimes we do not belong here.

What To Do?

Fortunately, there are many simple ways to ground ourselves:

Concentrating on our breathing.
Paying attention to the body.
Walking in a mindful way.
Being in nature.
Eating healthy food.
Anything that brings us back into our body is basically grounding, but it's also smart to know and practice grounding exercises that we can do quickly. At first, you should practice them with care, attention, and intention for a few minutes, but you can instantly ground faster after a while.

Energy: Ying

Zodiac: Cancer, Pisces, Scorpio, Taurus, Virgo
Solar System: Moon, Neptune, Venus
Rune:
Numbers: 1, 2, 4, 6, 7, 8, 10, 12
Color: Black
Tarot:
Trees: Apple, Beech, Birch, Cherry, Cypress, Elder, Elm, Horse Chestnut, Laurel, Magnolia, Mesquite, Mimosa, Myrtle, Palm, Poplar, Spindletree, Spruce, Sycamore, Willow, Yew
Misc. Plants: Aloe, Belladonna, Black Cohosh, Burdock, Cardamom, Coltsfoot, Cowslip, Dittany, Goldenrod, Henbane, Lady's Slipper, Lotus, Meadowsweet, Moonwort, Mullein, Myrrh, Orris Root, Patchouli, Reed, Sandalwood, Skullcap, Spikenard, Thornapple, Vanilla
Herb & Garden: Amaranth, Aster, Blackberry / Bramble, Catnip, Columbine, Comfrey, Daffodil, Daisy, Foxglove, Gardenia, Geranium, Grape, Heather, Hibiscus, Hyacinth, Iris, Ivy, Jasmine, Lady's Mantle, Lemon Balm, Lilac, Lily, Monkshood, Mugwort, Passionflower, Periwinkle, Poppy, Primrose, Raspberry, Rose, Sage, Solomon's Seal, Spearmint, Strawberry, Thyme, Valerian, Vervain Violet, Yarrow
Gemstones & Minerals: Agate (black with white veining, green, snakeskin, tree), Amazonite, Amethyst, Ametrine, Andalusite, Apophyllite, Aquamarine, Azurite, Beryl, Blue Lace Agate, Calcite, Celestite, Cerussite, Chrysocolla, Chrysoprase, Desert Rose, Diopside, Emerald, Iolite, Jade, Jasper (brown, green, ocean, pink), Jet, Kunzite, Labradorite, Lapis Lazuli, Larimar, Lepidolite, Lodestone, Malachite, Moonstone, Morganite, Moss Agate, Opal, Peridot, Petrified Wood, Quartz (blue, clear, green, tourmalated), Rose Quartz, Salt, Sapphire, Selenite, Smoky Quartz, Sodalite, Staurolite, Sugilite, Tourmaline (watermelon), Tsavorite, Turquoise
From the Sea: Coral, Cow, Mother-of-Pearl, Pearl
Metals: Copper, Lead, Mercury, Silver
Angel & Mythical Being: Dragon, Unicorn

Energy: Yang

Zodiac: Aquarius, Aries, Capricorn, Gemini, Leo, Libra, Sagittarius
Solar System: Mars, Pluto, Sun
Runes:
Numbers: 1, 3, 5, 7, 9, 11, 13
Color: White
Tarot:
Trees: Acacia, Alder, Ash, Aspen, Blackthorn, Cedar, Chestnut, Fir, Hawthorn, Hazel, Holly, Juniper, Linden, Locust, Maple, Oak, Olive, Palm (dragon's blood), Pine, Pomegranate, Rowan Walnut, Witch Hazel, Yew
Misc. Plants: Allspice, Anise, Asafoetida, Bamboo, Betony, Bittersweet, Blessed Thistle, Bloodroot, Cinnamon, Cinquefoil, Clove, Coriander, Cumin, Deer's Tongue, Eyebright, Flax, Frankincense, Galangal, Ginger, Ginseng, High John, Horehound, Mandrake, Mistletoe, Mustard, Nettle, Nutmeg, Pepper, Reed, Star Anise, Thistle, Wormwood
Herb & Garden: Agrimony, Anemone, Angelica, Basil, Bergamot, Borage, Broom, Carnation, Chamomile, Chrysanthemum, Clover, Dandelion, Dill, Fennel, Fern, Feverfew, Garlic, Goldenseal, Gorse, Heliotrope, Holy Basil, Honeysuckle, Lavender, Lily of the Valley, Lovage, Marigold, Marjoram, Morning Glory, Pennyroyal, Peony, Peppermint, Rosemary, Rue, Saffron, St. John's Wort, Snapdragon, Sunflower, Sweet Woodruff
Gemstones & Minerals: Agate (banded, black, brown, fire, red, red-banded, snakeskin), Amber, Amethyst, Ametrine, Andalusite, Apache Tears, Aventurine, Beryl (golden), Bloodstone, Calcite (orange, red), Carnelian, Cat's Eye, Chrysoberyl, Citrine, Diamond, Fluorite, Garnet, Hematite, Herkimer Diamond, Jasper (leopard skin, red, yellow), Lodestone, Obsidian, Onyx, Opal, Pyrite, Quartz (clear, rutilated), Rhodochrosite, Rhodonite, Ruby, Sard, Sardonyx, Serpentine, Sphene, Spinel, Staurolite, Sunstone, Tanzanite, Tiger's Eye, Topaz, Tourmaline (red, watermelon), Zircon
From the Sea: Coral (red)
Metals: Aluminum, Antimony, Brass, Gold, Iron, Mercury, Steel, Tin
Angel or Mythical Being: Dragon, Phoenix, Unicorn

Grounding Exercise 1

One of the easiest ways to ground is to bring your attention to the breath as it enters and leaves the body, not trying to change it in any way, just observing it. After about 10 breaths, you will probably find that you are more connected to your physical body. Then, bring your awareness to the sensations in your body, moving from your head down to your feet, exploring and inquiring as you work your way around the body. Just a few minutes of this can bring you home to your body and the Earth, which is what it means to ground ourselves.

Then, imagine that you have roots growing out of the soles of your feet, and imagine those roots flowing down into the Earth. The roots flow with us so we can always move, but at the same time, they keep us grounded. Imagine these roots flowing down through all of the layers of the Earth and connecting right down into the magnetic core of the planet (or however you see the center).

Then, feeling anchored to the planet's center, imagine the energy from there flowing up through these roots into the soles of your feet and then up your legs into your pelvic area and your root chakra. Feel it flow up through your sacral chakra, the solar plexus, and then the heart chakra. If you want to, you can ground all the way up to your crown chakra.

We receive powerful energy from the Earth just as we do from the forms of energy we associate with the sky, and our body is a tool that brings these two energies together. When we are grounded, we become a strong container in which our spirits can safely and productively dwell. This is why grounding every day, especially at the beginning of the day, is such a beneficial practice. Fortunately, it's as simple as bringing our conscious awareness to our bodies and the Earth on which we walk.

Grounding simply re-connects your body's energy with the energy of the Earth, and this is a good practice for everybody, as it's very refreshing and invigorating.

Chakra Energy

Each chakra is connected to the central energy channel in the spine, called the Sushumna, and is also connected to the idea and the Pingala, which are the yin and the yang energy channels crisscrossing along the Sushumna. The points where they cross are the locations of the seven major chakras.

The chakras act like transformers. They draw in and distribute subtle energy from the Universal supply of ki, and act as exit points for unwanted energy.

The chakras store the energy of thoughts, feelings, memories, experiences, and actions. They influence and direct our present and future mindset, behavior, emotional health, and activities.

Our energy system governs our energetic and psychic well-being.

The life force in each chakra can be processed, transmuted, and released so that we consciously manifest what we want to call in rather than experience more of the same. Prana informs us and influences our actions and behaviors, determining our health, career opportunities, relationships, etc. The subtle body depicts how our inner reality creates our outer reality.

Balancing Act

Your chakras are responsible for your health and well-being. You'll feel physically and emotionally good when they're balanced and healthy. However, when one or more of your chakras needs to be balanced, it can lead to problems. To keep your chakras balanced, ensure they're all spinning in the same direction and are the same size. Also, check that they're free of obstruction and appear bright.

When one of your chakras is blocked, it's not spinning as quickly or smoothly as the others. This can be due to a buildup of dense energies, making the chakra appear smaller than normal. In some cases, the chakra might spin in the opposite direction. If you have a blocked chakra, addressing the issue as soon as possible is important.

An overactive chakra is often spinning too quickly, appearing out of control. It may also appear larger than normal and begin to dominate the energy of neighboring chakras if left unbalanced. An overactive chakra can also change shape, becoming oval or oblong rather than a perfect circle.

Grounding Exercise 2

First, ensure you sit comfortably, relaxed, with your eyes closed and your feet flat on the floor. Focus on your breathing. Breathe in with your nose and out through your mouth.

Focus your attention on the bottom of your spine (root chakra).

Imagine that you are sending an anchor from your spine deep into the Earth on a very long rope or chain.

Allow it to drop deeper, maybe feeling that you are being pulled downwards or that your spine is being extended.

Focus on your feet and imagine dropping an anchor, long rope, or chain from each foot.

Again, allow them to drop deeper and deeper, and you may feel like your legs are pulling downwards.

Your legs may feel heavy, and your feet may feel as if they are stuck to the floor.
This feeling is good because it now means you are grounded – your body is heavy and relaxed.

Imagine the Earth's energy flowing into your root chakra and feel that connection to the Earth is both permanent and stable.

There are many grounding exercises. For example, you could imagine yourself as a tree, with roots deep into the Earth below you, with your legs and body as the trunk and arms and head as the branches.

Grounding Notes

Centering
Energy and Meditation

Learning to center yourself is a fundamental aspect of energy work and the very essence of magic. As most magic involves harnessing and manipulating energy, mastering centering should be one of your initial magical practices. Centering consists in focusing on the feeling and manipulation of energy while practicing meditative breathing. It is believed that centering unites the mind, body, and soul.

Energy Centering Exercise
It's important to find a peaceful and distraction-free space to meditate effectively. Once settled, take a seat on the ground and concentrate on your breath. Begin by rubbing your palms together as if you're trying to warm them up. Then, slowly pull your hands 1-2 inches apart and repeat the process.

Think of Centering as pulling energy.

Energy from Centering
When we Center, we are essentially drawing in energy.
During the Centering exercise, you may feel tingling or resistance. This is caused by the flow of energy through your body. Once you understand this, you can focus on the resistance and use visualization techniques to direct the energy throughout your body. It is advisable to start each Centering session with this exercise.

Energy Manipulation
When you clearly understand the energy sensation, you'll observe that it expands as you move your hands apart. I love stretching it out and creating a field with my hands by placing them about an inch away from the object I want to transfer the energy to, like a spell jar. Before starting the transfer, I always start with a Centering Exercise to get myself acquainted with the energy.

Helpful Tools:
Consider using crystals, music, incense, or whatever you feel works best for you.

Centering Notes

Shielding

Protection Energy

By now, you understand that Centering draws energy from the universe while Grounding pushes it away. The next step is Shielding, which involves using the entered energy to create a protective bubble that shields you from spiritual attacks and negative energy. To achieve this, you must first Center and then expand your energy.

Energy Shielding Exercise

To begin, it's best to find a peaceful and distraction-free space. Take a moment to focus your attention and connect with your inner energy. Envision this energy as a bright and vibrant light, and watch as it expands and grows. Imagine this light enveloping your entire body, creating a protective aura around you.
Think of shielding as creating an energy bubble.

Energy Shield

When you create an Energy Shield, it is advisable to imagine the outer layer as reflective. This will ensure that any negative energy aimed at you will be reflected instead of being absorbed.

When to Shield

waxing moon phase
before reading auras
before tarot readings
practicing magic with others
before going somewhere crowded
before scrying
after aligning chakras

Energy bubbles can keep your positive energy in as well as keep negative energy out.

Helpful Tools:

Consider using crystals, music, incense, or whatever you feel works best for you.

Shielding Notes

Self-Healing Your Chakras

You can use several tools and techniques to open, heal and balance your chakras.

Yoga Poses: Yoga is an excellent way to get your chakras to open up and help your energy flow freely throughout your body. Yoga helps to move stuck and stagnant energy from your energy field, which can prevent the chakras from functioning correctly. For example, if someone is having trouble opening their heart chakra, I recommend spending ten minutes a day doing back bending poses that help open their chest, heart, shoulders, and upper spine.

Essential Oils: Aromatherapy can be a helpful tool for recalibrating our thoughts, emotions, and energies. Scents containing earthy scents and tree properties can help the root chakra better align and focus a person's energy downward. This can be helpful for individuals who are struggling to keep their energy grounded.

Crystals: Healing crystals can balance, replenish and restore energy levels. People who love crystals also often like to bathe with them, infuse water with their energies, sleep with gemstones, or decorate their homes with rocks. When chakra healing, you can place a healing stone directly on or near the chakra you want to work with while meditating or resting.

Sounds: Singing bowls, tuning forks, and Solfeggio frequencies can be used to open and heal blocked chakras. Listening to certain sounds in nature can also be helpful. For example, listening to water sounds such as rain, waves, or waterfalls can help a person to connect more deeply to their sacral chakra and the watery properties of the womb.

Foods: Certain diets can help to open chakras or clear blocked energies. One example is eating more "yellow foods," such as peppers, lentils, squash, bananas, and/or corn, to assist with the healing of the solar plexus chakra.

Energy Work: You can do several daily things to help clear your energy and raise your vibration. This includes things like clearing your chakras and balancing your energy field. These activities can be beneficial in removing stuck energy and keeping yourself in balance.

Using A Pendulum To Check Your Chakras

Using a pendulum is one way to tell if your chakras are out of balance. This is a quick and easy way to check your chakras, and anyone can do it. To check your chakras with a pendulum, follow these steps:

Hold the pendulum in your dominant hand, and place it a few inches above the palm of your other hand.

Wait for the pendulum to stop moving, or command it to be still by saying "stop" out loud. Then, ensure the pendulum has always stopped moving before asking a new question.

Tell your pendulum: "Show me what a healthy chakra on my body looks like." Wait for the pendulum to respond and begin moving. Note the direction the chakra spins, how fast it spins, and how big of a circle it makes.

Once the pendulum has stopped moving, ask it to show you what each chakra looks like. For example, say: "Now, show me what my root chakra looks like." Then, take note of what the pendulum does. If it spins in the opposite direction, changes size, or barely moves, it could indicate a blockage in that chakra. It could mean an overactive chakra if it starts spinning faster, makes oblong shapes, or spins in a large circle.

Repeat this for each of your 7 main chakras.

Chakra Notes

Simplified Psychic Abilities

Clairvoyance - When you see stuff (clear vision)

Clairaudience - When you hear stuff (clear hearing)

Clairsentience - When you feel stuff (clear sensing and feeling)

Clairempathy - When you feel other people's stuff

Claircognizance - When you just know stuff (clear knowing)

Clairsgustance - When you taste stuff (clear taste)

Clairalience or Clairscent - When you smell stuff (clear smell)

Clairtangency /Pyschometry - When you get touched and stuff (clear touch)

Telepathy - When you can communicate through thoughts and stuff

Telekenisis - When you can move things with your mind and stuff

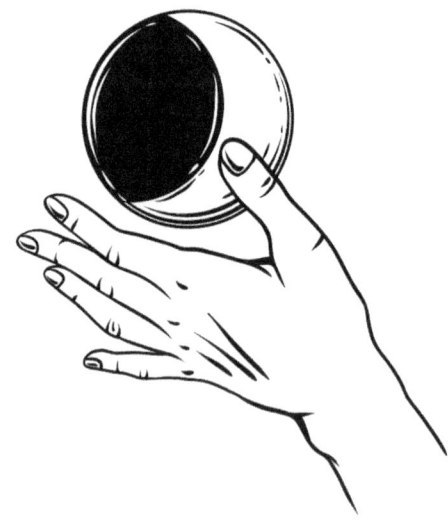

Types of Empaths

It's extremely rare to be an empath. Research estimates that just 1-2 percent of the population possesses empath traits.

Empaths tend to everyone else's needs before their own and tend to experience emotional burnout more than others.

Empaths are considered excellent listeners; people often approach them with their problems. They are also regarded as good problem-solvers and caring and nurturing individuals with unique abilities to feel or read people or situations, depending on their type.

Empaths are also very receptive and perceptive to their environment and the energy surrounding them.

These types of people will take on the world's problems if they can and carry that burden around with them — they are more prone to depression and chronic fatigue, due to their heightened emotional nature and inability to let others deal with their emotions on their own, with time.

Claircognizant/Intuitive Empath
Being a claircognizant or intuitive empath, you can know if and what must be done in a situation without any solid evidence or rationale.

Depending on the context and circumstances, this type of empath can know whether or not they should do something. Claircognizant empaths can vibe off of the energy field of others, and, having that ability, they can scan people.

Psychometric Empath
The psychometric empath can receive information and energy from objects, photographs, or locations that are significant to a person.

Psychometric empaths can also form impressions and relate situations or past events with inanimate objects. They can use the energy from a place or inanimate object to receive information and impressions about it.

Types of Empaths

Flora Empath

This type of empath can communicate with plants and receive their signals. A flora empath, also known as a plant empath, can sense what plants need and communicate more intimately with plants. As a result, they can use plants' energy to help plants stay alive, grow and prosper. For example, if plants are in danger, the flora empath can communicate this with the plants.

Fauna Empath

This pertains to the ability to feel and communicate with animals. Fauna empaths, also called animal empaths, can also send messages to animals.

Typically, communication is initiated by the empath and rarely by the animals. Those who hear these messages may realize that animals are requesting a change in the animal's life.

Geomantic Empath

A geomantic empath can read signs and get signals from the soil or earth. This empath is especially sensitive to reading and feeling future natural disasters.

Geomantic empaths can detect when natural disasters, such as hurricanes and earthquakes, will be hit by the earth's energy signals and changes in that energy.

Telepathic Empath

This type of empath can read another person's thoughts and feelings, even when they aren't vocalized or expressed by the person. This type of empath can read other people's thoughts, feelings, and beliefs using the five senses.

Telepathic empaths can also take objects and form impressions on feelings associated with the particular object.

Precognitive Empath

The precognitive empath can feel a situation or event occur before it happens. This can be seen through dreams of extreme emotional and physical upheaval.

Precognitive empaths may experience sudden anxiety and nervousness, and their intuition becomes intensified or heightened. This type of empath usually has heightened sensitivity.

Types of Empaths

Emotional Empath

Emotional empaths can read and feel the emotions of others.

While this is a common trait among empaths, in general, this type is especially sensitive to feeling and reading others' emotions without others having to explain what they are going through or why they are feeling a certain way.

Physical Empath

This type of empath can feel another person's pain and symptoms within their own body. Therefore, this type of empath is considered to be a medical empath.

Physically receptive empaths can feel another's complaints and know the amount of physical pain or discomfort they are in.

Medium or Psychic Empath

The medium empath can communicate, hear, and see different spirits. In addition, they can communicate with those who are no longer with us.

Medium empaths can sometimes see spirits and communicate one-on-one with them.

Heyoka Empath

The heyoka empath is the most powerful type of empath. Known in Native American culture as the "Sacred Clown," a heyoka tends to be unconventional in their thoughts and actions and act as emotional mirrors for those around them.

The heyoka empaths' ability to make people question themselves promotes emotional healing in those around them.

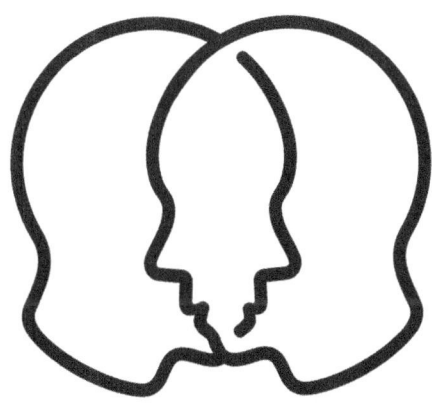

Archetypes

The term "archetype" means "original pattern" in ancient Greek. Jung used the concept of archetype in his theory of the human psyche. He identified 12 universal, mythic character archetypes that reside within our collective unconscious.

Jung defined twelve primary types that represent the range of basic human motivations. However, each of us tends to have one dominant archetype that dominates our personality.

The 12 Jungian Archetypes
Ruler
Creator/Artist
Sage
Innocent
Explorer
Rebel
Hero
Wizard
Jester
Everyman
Lover
Caregiver

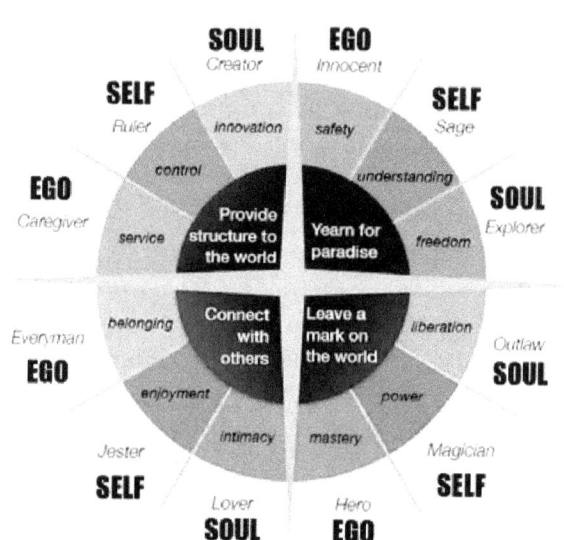

The 4 Cardinal Orientations

The 4 cardinal orientations that the archetypes are seeking to realize are:
Ego – Leave a Mark on the World.
Order – Provide Structure to the World.
Social – Connect to others.
Freedom – Yearn for Paradise.

The Ego Types

The Innocent
The Everyman/Regular Guy
The Hero
The Caregiver

The Soul Types

The Explorer
The Rebel
The Lover
The Creator/Artist

The Self Types

The Jester
The Sage
The Magician
The Ruler

Witch/Pretty Words

Agathist - a person who believes that all things tend toward an ultimate goal.

Agni - sacred reciprocity: the practice of living in harmony with the spirit of the earth.

Ailurophile - a person who loves felines: a cat lover.

Astrophilia - love of and/or obsession with planets, stars, and outer space.

Ataraxia - a state of serene calmness; the serenity of mind.

Ceraunophilia - loving thunder and lightning and finding them intensely beautiful.

Dadirri - a deep, spiritual act of reflective and respectful listening or communion with life.

Friscalating - shimmering on the horizon at sunset, an effect caused by the sun setting over the horizon, creating an optical illusion of shimmering, liquefied light akin to a mirage.

Hinterland - an area lying beyond what is visible or known.

Isolophilia - strong affection for solitude, being alone.

Meraki - to do something with soul, creativity, or love; to put something of yourself into your work.

Nefelibata - "cloud walker"; one who lives in the clouds of their own imagination or dreams or one who does not obey the conventions of society, literature, or art.

Oneiromancy -The practice of predicting the future through the interpretation of dreams.

Philocalist - a lover of beauty; someone who finds and appreciates beauty in all things.

Rutilant - glowing or glittering with ruddy or golden light.

Seraphine - passionate

Sonder - the realization that each passerby has a life as vivid and complex as your own.

Werifesteria - to wander longingly through the forest in search of mystery.

Witchery - the practice of magic, witchcraft, and compelling power.

Yugen - a profound awareness of the universe that triggers feelings too deep and mysterious for words.

And just for fun:

Witchuation - Witch-uation - a situation that requires one or more witches to conjure and solve a problem or issue.

Witch Words Notes:

Spirituality vs. Religion

Spirituality is not religion. Religions are systems of attitudes, beliefs, and practices that focus on groups, while spirituality centers on an individual's understanding of their place in the world.

Spirituality does not come from religion. It comes from our soul. Therefore, we must stop confusing religion and spirituality. Religion is a set of rules, regulations, and rituals humans create to help people spiritually. Spirituality is not theology or ideology. It is simply a way of life, pure and original, as given by the Most High. Spirituality is a network linking us to God/Our Most Highest Self/Source, the universe, and each other.

Omnism

Omnism is the recognition and respect of all religions and their gods or lack thereof. Those who hold this belief are called omnists, sometimes written as omniest. In recent years, the term has been resurfacing due to the increased interest of modern-day self-described omnists who have rediscovered and begun to redefine the term. Omnism is similar to syncretism. Syncretism is the combining of different beliefs and various schools of thought. Syncretism involves the merging or assimilation of several originally discrete traditions, especially in the theology and mythology of religion, thus asserting an underlying unity and allowing for an inclusive approach to other faiths. However, it can also be seen as a way to accept the existence of various religions without believing in all they profess to teach. Many omnists say that all religions contain truths, but no one religion offers all that is truth.

Elemental Magic

The elements are another essential aspect of Witchcraft; we often call on them during spells and rituals. There are four primary elements, each of which has particular associations. Each element represents a different type of energy that you can harness.

Earth Magic - The element of Earth is the foundation of all life. The color green and the northern quarter align with the element of Earth. It is potent in spells that require wisdom and spells for fertility, prosperity, strength, and wealth.

Air Magic - The element of air is light fuel for all living things. It is represented by the color yellow and the eastern quarter when casting a circle. Spells for renewal, change, intuition, and knowledge call upon the air.

Fire Magic - The element of fire is a source of creation and destruction of life. It is represented by the color red and the southern quarter when casting a circle. Spells for passion, inspiration, intuition, creativity, and protection use fire.

Water Magic - Water represents the flow of life. It is represented by the color blue and the western quarter when casting a circle. It is powerful in spells for healing, peace, and compassion.

Earth

Symbol: ▽

Numbers: 4, 6, 8

Solar System: Earth, Saturn, and Venus

Zodiac: Capricorn, Taurus, and Virgo

Celebrations: Earth Day, Hunting of the Wren, and Yule

Season: Winter

Time of Day: Midnight

Runes: Is, Tyr, and Ur

Ogham: Ioho

Tarot: Pentacles

Direction: North

Sense: Touch

Energy: Yin

Chakra: Root

Colors: Black, Brown, Green, and White

Trees: Ash, Blackthorn, Cedar, Cypress, Elder, Elm, Holly, Juniper, Locust, Magnolia, Maple, Oak, Olive, Pine, Pomegranate, Rowan, Spruce, and Witch Hazel

Herbs & Flowers: Comfrey, Fern, Honeysuckle, Ivy, Jasmine, Mugwort, Primrose, Sage, and Vervain

Misc. Plants: Cinquefoil, Clove, Grains, Henbane, High John, Horehound, Mandrake, Patchouli, and Reed

Gemstones & Minerals: Agate, Alexandrite, Amazonite, Amber, Andalusite, Apophyllite, Calcite (green), Cat's Eye, Cerussite, Chrysocolla, Chrysoprase, Diopside, Emerald, Fluorite, Hematite, Jade, Jasper, Jet, Kunzite, Malachite, Moss Agate, Peridot, Petrified Wood, Quartz (rutilated), Salt, Smoky Quartz, Staurolite, Sugilite, Tourmaline (black, brown, green, watermelon), Turquoise, and Unakite

Metals: Lead and Mercury

From the Sea: Coral (black)

Earth

Angels: Gabriel and Auriel

Goddesses: Anat, Ariadne, Artemis, Asherah, Bertha, Ceres, Demeter, Gaia, Kore, Nephthys, Persephone, Rhea, and Rhiannon

Gods: Adonis, Arawn, Cernunnos, Dionysus, Geb, the Green Man, Khnum, Marduk, Mimir, Pan, Prometheus and Vishnu

Magical Beings: Brownies, Dryads, Elves, Fairies, Gnomes, Pixies

Animals: Antelope, Armadillo, Badger, Bear, Boar, Buffalo / Bison, Cattle, Deer (stag), Dog, Elephant, Goat, Groundhog, Hippopotamus, Jaguar, Mole, Otter, Pig, Prairie Dog, and Wolverine.

Birds: Blue Jay, Chicken, Crow, Goose, Sparrow, Swan, Turkey, and Woodpecker

Reptiles: Crocodile, Snake, Toad, Tortoise, and Turtle

Insect/Misc: Dragonfly

Mythical: Dragon and Selkies

Ritual Tool: Pentacle

Principle: To Be Silent

Issues, Intentions & Powers: abundance, acceptance, agriculture, anxiety, balance, beginnings, business, comfort, communication, consecrate/bless, consciousness, creativity, cycles, death, endurance, energy (general, receptive), family, fertility, gentleness, grounding, growth, healing, hexes, the home, justice, life, magic (dragon), manifestation, money, nurture, the otherworld/underworld, patience, peace, pregnancy/childbirth, prosperity, protection, purpose, rebirth/renewal, relationships, the senses (smell, touch), sensuality, sexuality, spirits (nature spirits), stability, strength, success, support, travel, warmth, wealth, weather, well-being, willpower, and wisdom

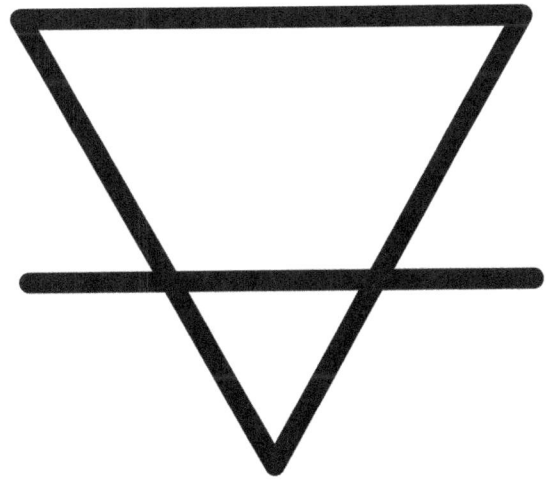

Air

Symbol: △
Number: 5
Solar System: Jupiter, Mercury, and Uranus
Zodiac: Aquarius, Gemini, and Libra
Celebration: Ostara
Season: Spring
Time of Day: Dawn
Runes: Beorc, Hagal, and Thorn
Ogham: Onn
Tarot: Fool, Swords, and Wands
Direction: East
Sense: Smell
Energy: Yang
Chakras: Crown, Heart, and Throat
Colors: Blue (light), Gray, Lavender, Pink, Red, Silver, White, and Yellow (bright, light)
Trees: Acacia, Alder, Apple, Ash, Aspen, Cedar, Chestnut, Elder, Elm Fir, Hawthorn, Hazel, Holly, Horse Chestnut, Laurel, Linden, Maple, Mesquite, Oak, Olive, Palm, Pine, Sycamore, Walnut, and Yew
Herbs & Flowers: Agrimony, Anemone, Bergamot, Borage, Broom, Clover, Comfrey, Dandelion, Fern, Ivy, Lavender, Lily of the Valley, Marjoram, Marigold, Mugwort, Peppermint, Primrose, Sage, Spearmint, Thyme, Vervain, Violet, and Yarrow
Misc. Plants: Anise, Bamboo, Bittersweet, Eyebright, Frankincense, Goldenrod, Horehound, Meadowsweet, Mistletoe, Myrrh, Nutmeg, Reed, Sandalwood, Star Anise, and Wormwood
Gemstones & Minerals: Agate (tree), Ametrine, Angelite, Aragonite, Aventurine, Blue Lace Agate, Celestite, Chrysoberyl, Desert Rose, Moldavite, Opal, Quartz (clear), Sodalite, Sphene, Staurolite, Topaz (blue), and Tourmaline (blue)
Metals: Aluminum, Mercury, and Tin
From the Sea: Angel Wing and Jingle

Air

Angels: Michael and Raphael
Goddesses: Amaterasu, Athena, Arianrhod, Hera, Nut, and Phoebe
Gods: Hermes, Khnum, Mimir, Mercury, Quetzalcoatl, Thoth, and Zeus
Magical Beings: Elves, Fairies, Pixies
Animal: Gazelle
Birds: Albatross, Condor, Eagle, Falcon, Hawk, and Seagull
Reptile:
Insect/Misc.: Firefly
Mythical: Dragon, Sphinx, and Thunderbird
Ritual Tools: Athame, Incense, and Sword
Principle: To Know
Issues, Intentions & Powers: acceptance, action, Astral Realm, beginnings, business, clairvoyance, clarity, communication, concentration/ focus, consecrate/bless, creativity, divination, enchantment, energy, enlightenment, fairness, freedom, harmony, healing, imagination, inspiration, intelligence, intuition, justice, knowledge, learning, life, light, loss, magic (animal, dragon), memory/memories, the mind, money, motivation, order/ organize, power, protection, psychic ability, purification, relationships, release, the senses (hearing, smell, touch), shamanic work, spirits, spirituality, travel, visions, weather (general, lightning, storms), willpower, and wisdom

Fire

Symbol: △
Numbers: 1, 3, 9
Solar System: Jupiter, Mars, and Sun
Zodiac: Aries, Leo, and Sagittarius
Celebrations: Beltane, Imbolc, and Litha
Season: Summer
Time of Day: Midday
Runes: Dag, Ken, Rad, and Sigel
Ogham: Ur
Tarot: Judgement, Swords, and Wands
Direction: South
Sense: Sight
Energy: Yang
Chakra: Solar Plexus
Colors: Crimson, Gold, Orange, Pink, Red, White, and Yellow
Trees: Alder, Ash, Beech, Blackthorn, Cedar, Cherry, Chestnut, Elder, Hawthorn, Holly, Horse Chestnut, Juniper, Laurel, Mesquite, Oak, Olive, Palm (dragon's blood), Pine, Pomegranate, Rowan, Walnut, Willow, Witch Hazel, and Yew
Herbs & Flowers: Amaranth, Anemone, Angelica, Basil, Carnation, Chrysanthemum, Dill, Fennel, Garlic, Goldenseal, Gorse, Heliotrope, Hibiscus, Holy Basil, Lovage, Marigold, Pennyroyal, Peony, Peppermint, Poppy, Primrose, Rosemary, Rue, St. John's Wort, Snapdragon, Sunflower, Sweet Woodruff, and Vervain
Misc. Plants: Allspice, Asafetida, Betony, Black Cohosh, Blessed Thistle, Bloodroot, Cinnamon, Cinquefoil, Clove, Coriander, Cumin, Deer's Tongue, Flax, Frankincense, Galangal, Ginger, Ginseng, High John, Mandrake, Mullein, Mustard, Nettle, Nutmeg, Pepper, Thistle, and Wormwood
Gemstones & Minerals: Agate (banded, black, brown, fire, red, red-banded, snakeskin), Amber, Amet-rine, Apache Tears, Beryl (golden), Bloodstone, Calcite (orange, red), Carnelian, Citrine, Diamond, Garnet, Hematite, Herkimer Diamond, Jasper (red), Obsidian, Onyx, Opal (fire), Peridot, Pyrite, Quartz, Rhodochrosite, Rhodonite, Ruby, Sard, Sardonyx, Serpentine, Smoky Quartz, Spinel, Staurolite, Sunstone, Tiger's Eye, Topaz, Tourmaline (red), Tsavorite, and Zircon (red)
Metals: Antimony, Brass, Gold, Iron, and Steel
From the Sea: Coral (red)

Fire

Angel: Michael
Goddesses: Aine, Amaterasu, Bertha, Brigid, Danu, Durga, Freya, Hestia, Kupala, Pele, Phoebe, Sekhmet, Spider-Woman, and Vesta
Gods: Agni, Belenus, Brahma, Dionysus, Hephaestus, Horus, Inari, Indra, Khnum, Mimir, Nergal, Nord, Perun, Prometheus, and Vulcan
Magical Beings: Mermaids and Salamanders
Animals: Goat, Hedgehog, Horse, Lion, Porcupine, Sheep (ram), and Tiger
Birds: Crane, Eagle, Falcon, Heron, Macaw, Peacock, Quail, Robin, Swallow, Woodpecker, and Wren
Reptiles: Lizard, Salamander, and Snake
Insects/Misc.: Bee, Cicada, Firefly, Ladybug, Praying Mantis, and Scorpion
Mythical: Dragon and Phoenix
Ritual Tools: Censer and Wand
Principle: To Will
Issues, Intentions & Powers: action, activate/awaken, ambition, anger, authority, battle/war, cheerfulness, communication, concentration/ focus, confidence, consecrate/bless, courage, creativity, defense, desire, destruction, divination, energy, faith, freedom, healing, honor, illumination, influence, inspiration, intelligence, intuition, justice, leadership, life, light, love, lust, magic (general, defensive, dragon, sex), the mind, motivation, passion, power, protection, psychic ability, purification, purity, purpose, release, revenge, sexuality, stimulation, transformation, truth, warmth, weather (general, lightning), and willpower

Water

Symbol: ▽
Numbers: 2, 7
Solar System: Mercury, Moon, Neptune, Pluto, and Saturn
Zodiac: Cancer, Pisces, and Scorpio
Celebrations: Mabon and Neptunalia
Season: Autumn
Time of Day: Dusk
Runes: Feoh, Jera, Lagu, and Peorth
Ogham: Eadha, and Eamhancholl
Tarot: Cups, Hanged Man, and Moon
Direction: West
Sense: Taste
Energy: Yin
Chakra: Sacral
Colors: Aqua, Black, Blue, Gray, Green (blue, sea), Indigo, Lilac, Purple, Silver, Turquoise, Violet, and White
Trees: Alder, Apple, Ash, Aspen, Beech, Birch, Cedar, Cherry, Chestnut, Cypress, Elder, Elm, Hazel, Horse Chestnut, Locust, Magnolia, Mesquite, Mimosa, Myrtle, Olive, Poplar, Spindle-tree, Spruce, Sycamore, Willow, Witch Hazel, and Yew
Herbs & Flowers: Aster, Blackberry / Bramble, Catnip, Chamomile, Columbine, Comfrey, Daffodil, Daisy, Feverfew, Foxglove, Gardenia, Geranium, Grape, Heather, Hibiscus, Hyacinth, Iris, Ivy, Jasmine, Lady's Mantle, Lemon Balm, Lilac, Lily, Monkshood, Morning Glory, Passionflower, Periwinkle, Poppy, Raspberry, Rose, Solomon's Seal, Spearmint, Strawberry, Thyme, Valerian, Violet, and Yarrow
Misc. Plants: Aloe, Belladonna, Burdock, Cardamom, Coltsfoot, Cowslip, Dittany, Henbane, Lady's Slipper, Lotus, Meadowsweet, Moonwort, Myrrh, Orris Root, Reed, Sandalwood, Skullcap, Spikenard, Star Anise, Thornapple, Vanilla, and Water Lily
Gemstones & Minerals: Alexandrite, Amethyst, Ametrine, Angelite, Aquamarine, Aragonite, Azurite, Beryl, Blue Lace Agate, Calcite, Charoite, Chrysocolla, Dioptase, Fluorite, Jade, Jasper (ocean), Jet, Kyanite, Labradorite, Lapis Lazuli, Larimar, Lepidolite, Lodestone, Moonstone, Morganite, Obsidian (gold sheen), Opal, Quartz, Rose Quartz, Sapphire, Selenite, Sodalite, Staurolite, Sugilite Topaz (blue), Tourmaline (black, blue, pink, watermelon), Tsavorite, Turquoise, and Zircon (blue)
Metals: Copper, Mercury, and Silver
From the Sea: Coral, Mother-of-Pearl, and Pearl

Water

Angels: Raphael

Goddesses: Amphitrite, Aphrodite, Bad, Boann, Brigantia, Chalchiuhtlicue, Coventina, Isis, Kupala, Ran, Sarasvati, Sedna, and Tiamat

Gods: Aegir, Belenus, Ea, Khnum, Mabon, Manannan, Mimir, Neptune, Njord, Osiris, Poseidon, and Prometheus

Magical Beings: Mermaids, Norns, and Undines

Animals: Bat, Beaver, Cattle (cow), Dog, Hare, Hippopotamus, Horse, Moose, Otter, Polar Bear, and Raccoon

Birds: Albatross, Blackbird, Cormorant, Crane, Dove, Duck, Heron, Kingfisher, Seagull, Stork, Swan, Swift, and Vulture

Reptiles: Crocodile, Frog, Salamander, Snake, and Toad

Insect/Misc.: Dragonfly

Mythical: Dragon and Selkies

Ritual Tools: Cauldron, Chalice, and Cup

Principle: To Dare

Issues, Intentions & Powers: adaptability, agriculture, balance, beginnings, change/s, clairvoyance, compassion, consecrate/bless, consciousness (subconscious), creativity, desire, divination, dream work, emotions, empathy, energy (general, psychic, receptive), fertility, friendship, grace, growth, healing, heartbreak, influence, introspection, intuition, life, magic (animal, dragon, moon), memory /memories, nurture, patience, power, pregnancy/childbirth, protection, psychic ability, purification, purity, rebirth/ renewal, reconciliation, reversal, secrets, sensitivity, sensuality, shamanic work, sleep, sorrow, spirituality, strength (inner), stress, transformation, weather (general, storms), well-being, and wisdom

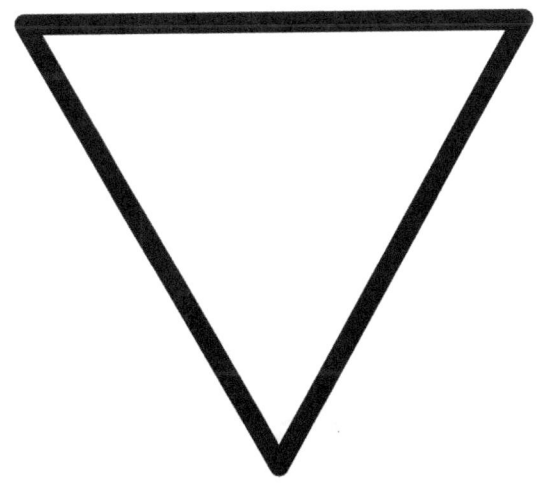

Element Spell Jars

Air
Star Anise
Mint
Lavender
Lemongrass
Salt
Flourite
Amethyst

Earth
Mugwort
Patchouli
Corn Kernels
Primrose
Some dirt of your choosing
Unakite
Tiger's Eye

Fire
Cloves
Rosemary
Pepper Flakes
Calendula
Red Salt
Garnet
Carnelian

Water
Chamomile
Roses
Eucalyptus
Sea Salt
Aquamarine
Lapis Lazuli

How to personalize your spell jar
Include handwritten intentions, sigils, or doodles
Add an inspiring quote or poetry
Use several items that resonate with you
Use locally grown herbs and flowers that you have foraged
Personal things related to your desired outcome

Symbols

Symbols have played a significant role throughout history, serving as a means of communication, expression, and identity. From ancient to modern times, symbols have been used to represent abstract concepts, convey religious beliefs, and create social cohesion. They have been etched into cave walls, inscribed on tablets, and emblazoned on flags. The power of symbols lies in their ability to capture the essence of an idea in a single image. They can evoke strong emotions, inspire action, and unite people across cultures and languages. The cross, for example, represents both religious devotion and colonial domination. Symbols are not static, they evolve with society, and their meanings can change. Symbols remain a crucial aspect of communication, and understanding their meaning and context is important for comprehending the complex ways in which humans communicate.

Evil Eye

The concept of the evil eye has a long-standing history in various cultures and belief systems across the globe. It suggests that certain individuals possess the power to cast a harmful gaze or send negative energy towards others, which can bring misfortune, illness, or harm to the recipient. The evil eye is often associated with emotions like jealousy, envy, or intense negative feelings. To safeguard against its influence, different societies have developed various talismans, amulets, or rituals to ward off the evil eye's effects. These protective measures can range from wearing specific symbols or charms to performing prayers or rituals for purification and defense. Despite its ancient origins, the concept of the evil eye still remains intriguing and continues to enthrall the imagination of many today.

Evil Eye Colors

Purple
General protection
To use your imagination to its fullest
To re-balance your life
To remove obstacles
To calm overactivity
To energize from depression

White
Purity, virginity, and protection
To clear clutter and obstacles away
To start a fresh beginning
To bring about mental clarity
Purification of thoughts or actions

Transparent
Clarity, mindfulness, and sanity protection
To comply with a neutral, non-invasive feeling

Evil Eye Colors

Dark Blue
Karma and Fate protection
Calm and relaxation to counteract chaos
To open the flow of communication

Brown
Elements protection
A solid wholesome feeling
To blend with the background
A connection with natural earth and the stability this brings
Orderliness and convention

Orange
Happiness protection
To spice things up when you feel that time is dragging
To become more involved in something
To increase creativity
Relief from things becoming too serious

Red
Courage protection
Increased enthusiasm
Interest in more energy action
Confidence to go after your dreams
Protection from fears and anxieties

Yellow
Health protection, clarity
For decision-making
Relief from burnout, panic, nervousness, exhaustion
Sharper memory and concentration skills
Protection from lethargy and depression

Light Blue
General protection
Broaden your perspective
Learning new information
Solitude and peace

Evil Eye Colors

Dark Green
Happiness protection
New state of balance
Feel a need for change or growth
Freedom to pursue new ideas
Protection from fears and anxieties
Connected with the demands of other

Pink
Friendship protection
Calm feelings
To neutralize disorder
Relaxation acceptance
Contentment

Violet
True love protection
To focus on personal issues
To develop intuition
To step outside of everyday life for a new and interesting way of viewing a problem
Solitude and inner communication

Grey
Sorrow and security protection
To emphasize your willingness
To reduce the intense energy of another color
To feel detached or isolated

Black
Power, prosperity, and protection
To become inconspicuous
To open the door to mystery
To prepare for the unknown
A restful emptiness

Light Green
Success protection
Increased personal power
Relaxation and enjoyment of life
Good health

What exactly is a spirit guide?

Spirit guides are nonhuman or human entities that reside in the spiritual realm and make their wisdom available to the living. They take various forms, including guardian angels, animal or nature spirits, elves and fairies, saints or ascended masters, and ancestors or descendants who have crossed the spiritual realm. According to believers, spiritual guides assist humans in their daily lives even though they are unaware of the guides' presence. Those interested are encouraged to seek out their guides to gain practical and mystical information, healing abilities, and protection from harm.

So here are my thoughts:
If you take comfort in believing in spirit guides, go right ahead and do it. Once again:

Live your life!
You Do You Boo!

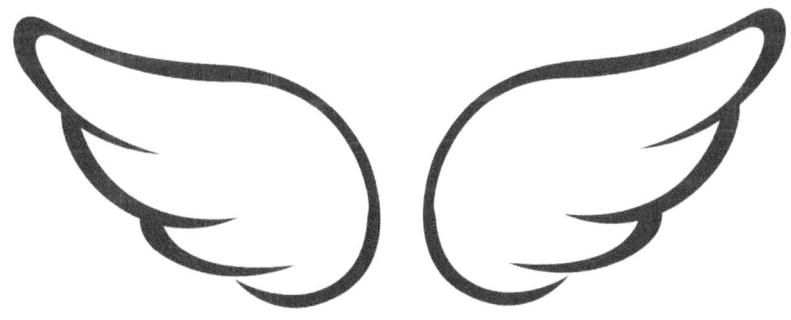

Types of Spirit Guides

Ascended Masters
Humans like us but who have transcended the
spiritual plane (ex: Buddha)

Star Beings
Star beings are galactic entities whom you may
have already known from the past

Animal Spirit Guides
Totems or Power Animals that provide healing
& support during tough times

Nature Spirits
Ethereal personifications of nature who have
come since the beginning of time

Ancestral Guides
They are spirit guides coming directly
from our genetic lineage

Angelic Spirit Guides
More commonly known as your
guardian angel

Elementals
Spirits who possess earthly elements, such as
Earth, water, fire, and air

Who's Who

Spirit Companion
These spirits have chosen to form a close relationship with a human friend. They generally seek a practitioner they feel can form a bond or companionship. They are not guides or teachers; however, they may fill those roles for their practitioners if they choose to do so. Most companions are found during the natural course of a spirit worker's spiritual journey or even through spirit adoption.

Spirit Guardians
These spirits choose to protect a person, place, or item. Guardians may be assigned to an individual at birth or during different times in their life. An individual may also seek them out. In times of danger, a guardian may be called upon to help keep their practitioner safe.

Spirit Guides
There are a few different types of spirit guides. Lifetime guides are those an individual will have with them their entire lives. These guides generally appear and are assigned at birth. Depending on several factors, they may choose to leave when death occurs or continue with the individual. Temporary or short-term guides will show up from time to time in an individual's life.

Spirit Familiars
Familiar spirits have a special connection with a practitioner. They can take on one or many different forms and aid the practitioner. They share a bond regarding their craft. They also can provide companionship and protection.

Animal Guides at a Glance

Elements: A strong connection to Mother Earth, playful humor, easy to relate to and connect with.
Talents: Alignment with our inner nature, protection, and enhanced instincts.
Traits: You're protective of family and community, physically oriented, and strongly connected to the natural environment.

Nature Spirits at a Glance

Elements: Playful creativity, manifestation skills, and the ability to heal the physical world (including our bodies and the environment).
Talents: Lightheartedness, a strong bond with animals, and a natural talent for magic.
Traits: You have a natural sense for power places and ley lines; you make an excellent peaceful warrior for the environment and are a natural healer.

Ascended Masters at a Glance

Elements: A wealth of knowledge about life on Earth, compassion for the human journey, the ability to connect people with their higher self
Talents: Discernment, wisdom, and gratitude.
Traits: You're a great teacher; you have lots of knowledge from past lives and a strong sense of responsibility.

Soul Symbols

The symbols of the soul are associated with one's birth month, and each represents distinct personality traits. You may gain insight into your natural behaviors by discovering your soul symbol and understanding its characteristics. Are you aware of your birth month? If so, you're about to discover your unique soul symbol, as each month has its own symbol with its own set of traits.

Soul Symbols

Month	Symbol	Description
January	Dragon	You possess a strong will and the ability to overcome any obstacle that may arise.
February	Pheonix	Your strength is derived from your incredible tenacity.
March	Yin-Yang	You strive to maintain a balance in all aspects of life and carefully evaluate the pros and cons of every situation.
April	Lion	You possess an immense passion within you.
May	Wolf	You are always there for the ones you love.
June	Fish	You exude the carefree spirit of the ocean and prioritize relishing in freedom and enjoyment.
July	Fire	When you have a passion, you pursue it wholeheartedly and commit to it without hesitation.
August	Horse	You are a free-spirited individual like a wild horse, always seeking new adventures and exploring your surroundings.
September	Flower	You have a truly pure and joyful heart that radiates positivity wherever you go.
October	Star	Your goal is to uplift others and assist them in achieving their aspirations.
November	Tree	You are a dependable source of assistance for those around you. Similar to a tree, you offer protection and sustenance to others.
December	Water	Just like water, your reactions can be fluid and adaptable in different situations, always changing and evolving.

Animal Guide

Elephant

The appearance of a fruit fly often signifies the need to adapt and persevere through difficult times. Fruit flies can represent transformation, rebirth, and the ability to view life uniquely, noticing even the tiniest details. Given their varied eye colors, fruit flies remind us to approach situations with an open mind and see things from multiple angles. Like the resilient little fruit fly, we all have the capacity for survival, even during times of decay or uncertainty.

If you encounter a fruit fly, it may be time to make positive changes in your life without hesitation or doubt. Don't shy away from taking action- embrace it! Fruit flies are powerful symbols that reveal your inner strength and resilience in challenging circumstances. They also help restore harmony in strained relationships by promoting peaceful communication and forgiveness.

Fruit Fly

The appearance of a fruit fly often signifies the need to adapt and persevere through difficult times. Fruit flies can represent transformation, rebirth, and the ability to view life uniquely, noticing even the tiniest details. Given their varied eye colors, fruit flies remind us to approach situations with an open mind and see things from multiple angles. Like the resilient little fruit fly, we all have the capacity for survival, even during times of decay or uncertainty.

If you encounter a fruit fly, it may be time to make positive changes in your life without hesitation or doubt. Don't shy away from taking action- embrace it! Fruit flies are powerful symbols that reveal your inner strength and resilience in challenging circumstances. They also help restore harmony in strained relationships by promoting peaceful communication and forgiveness.

Kangaroo

The kangaroo symbolizes overcoming obstacles, staying grounded, and moving forward. It's important not to dwell on or have regrets about past choices. Like the kangaroo's sturdy feet, you have a strong foundation that keeps you personally and spiritually steady. When self-doubt arises, remember your truth and believe in yourself.

It's crucial to lean on those closest to you during difficult times for support. They can help you be your best self. The meaningful direction of your life may change soon, but stay focused on the present moment. Instead of battling the opposition directly, try going around or over it as needed for momentum forward. Negative thoughts have no place in the kangaroo's world; always leap towards positivity and stay true to what matters most on your journey toward success.

Animal Guide

Lion
The animal totem of the Lion symbolizes leadership. When this spirit animal appears in your life, it could be a sign that you are (or about to be) in a position where you must take charge and dominate. This also extends to the professional realm: if you're finding yourself at the helm of a new endeavor, then the Lion is here to remind you to lead, delegate (don't try to do everything yourself), as well as learn from those around you - for example, taking cues on how best to bring harmony among peers by being an effective teacher - all while balancing work with your home life. On another level, this spirit guiding can assist when it seems like work is not getting done; Lion's presence encourages assertiveness and courage when facing challenges head-on becomes necessary. Overall, the Lion warns if a situation gets out of hand or threatens your mental and emotional well-being.

Manatee
Incorporating the symbol of the gentle manatee, embracing your emotions, and being in touch with them is crucial for moving forward. You create a deeper emotional self-awareness by acknowledging your feelings through writing, creating art, or simply reflecting on how you truly feel about situations.

You can achieve greatness by accepting yourself and others and believing that situations outside your control can be overcome. Manatee represents faith in oneself to reach the destination one desires, even if it takes longer than anticipated. Trusting in yourself is key to unlocking all that lies within you. Let the manatee guide you toward reaching your full potential by nurturing your inner self.

Pegasus
Pegasus, a divine stallion with wings, was known for bringing lightning and thunderbolts from Olympus to Zeus. Pegasus is significant as a symbol of spiritual growth, service to others, and travel. When Pegasus appears, it indicates your intention to pursue knowledge in the spiritual realm and elevate your soul's journey beyond the physical world. In Greek mythology, an inspirational spring was born every time Pegasus struck his hoof on the ground.

Pegasus represents the innate ability within you to transform negative situations into positive ones through spiritual connection. You possess gentleness, gracefulness, and emotional stability that attracts people toward you. They perceive you as genuine, transparent, and willing to listen attentively without judgment or bias. Your impartial guidance inspires them to uplift their spirituality.

However, it is important not to manipulate or take advantage of situations or people for personal gain nor blame others for one's actions, as it goes against what Pegasus stands for. Instead, let him assist you in finding inspiration when needed.

Animal Guide

Penguin

Penguins are highly symbolic creatures, particularly regarding spiritual growth and self-discovery. When a penguin appears in your life, it's a clear sign that you still have much to learn and explore on your spiritual journey. These birds offer hidden knowledge and insights to help you become more spiritually aware, especially through meditation and dreaming.

Penguin is also known for its nurturing nature. This means you strongly desire to care for others, especially the young and vulnerable. You enjoy teaching them how to be responsible and independent adults.

Unlike many animals, penguins aren't afraid of humans. They approach us with interest rather than fear, indicating that you, too, have an insatiable curiosity about the world around you. However, this trait can get you into trouble if you're not careful!

Flightless yet agile swimmers, penguins are symbols of groundedness, balance, security in oneself, and the ability to dive deep in search of knowledge. They encourage us to explore new ideas and perspectives with courage and determination.

Finally, if you are going through difficult transitions or feel like everything has been taken away, remember these situations are temporary. With hope and perseverance - qualities embodied by the resilient penguin - things will eventually return to normal.

Animal Guide

Phoenix

The Phoenix symbolizes renewal and transformation, representing the cycle of life from birth to death to rebirth. It signifies the ability to overcome challenges and return even stronger. When people say they will rise from the ashes like the Phoenix, they believe they will overcome tough times and emerge with greater resilience.

The Phoenix represents survival at its finest, embodying internal transformation and regeneration. Those who connect with this powerful symbol often experience heightened spiritual awareness, intuition, a sense of connection with all living things, and unwavering faith in the universe.

The Phoenix appears most often during times of transition when doors may close but new windows are about to open. If you're going through a period of change or upheaval, know that you are about to experience a time of rebirth. Let go of what no longer serves you and embrace new possibilities. Trust your inner wisdom and stay true to yourself as you navigate this process.

Remember that everything happens for a reason; even in the darkest moments, there is always hope for the future. Stay strong in your convictions, hold fast to your beliefs, and believe that light will always prevail over darkness.

Snail

The snail is a symbol of patience and resilience. When it appears, you may feel like your patience is being tested to the brink of breaking point. However, the snail reminds you that perseverance will ultimately pay off. You will overcome obstacles by focusing on the result and trusting in yourself and others.

The snail also serves as a protector against negative energies. You possess a heightened awareness of your surroundings, allowing you to stay on guard without being paranoid. While you may prefer solitude over crowds, embracing trust and balance is key during this period.

If snail symbolism resonates, consider raising your vibration to adapt easily to new situations. Trusting others can be challenging but ultimately rewarding for progress toward personal growth.

Animal Guide

Unicorn

The unicorn holds deep symbolic meaning, representing traits such as purity, faith, intuition, and enchantment. A connection to the higher realms of spirituality is embodied within this magnificent creature. It represents a pure heart and a gentle nature – the epitome of all that is right within the universe. Unicorns are also associated with inner peace, tranquility, righteousness, and steadfast belief in unseen things.

Unicorns often appear when individuals must delve deeper into their essence, connecting with their inner being or higher self. Consider it a sign that spirit guides are reaching out to you if you encounter one. Take pause when you see a unicorn – listen telepathically for any messages meant exclusively for you. Trust your instincts and believe everything will work out according to universal plans. Connecting with unicorns means opening yourself up to creative potential and embracing the mystical unknown while having confidence in your psychic abilities.

Encountering unicorns signals a time for spiritual growth, an opportunity to unlock the secrets of the universe's mysteries. With a pure heart connected to Divinity, unicorns incite wonderment and awe within us all.

Vulture

When the vulture appears, it's time to equalize things in your life. Vulture means looking past outward appearances to see the unique individual inside.

There's a story that when the sun got too close to Earth, a vulture pushed it away using its head and mighty wings.

The feathers were burned off of his head as he saved the world. This story means that someone can have a great strength of character inside and reasons for their outward appearance. If you don't take the time to know others, you're missing out on making a wonderful new friend.

Vulture is an expert in cleanliness. When it appears, it means removing all of the clutter from your home and work environment, letting go of all the excess baggage in your personal life, and letting go of any clutter in your mind that is causing you excessive stress. Vulture enables you to see the good in people, make the best out of a difficult situation, and encourages you to always look for the silver lining. It assists when you need purity of mind, body, and spirit.

Animal Guide

Woodpecker

The woodpecker symbolizes opportunity, reminding us to be aware when opportunity knocks. It encourages us to find creative and unique ways to solve problems and figure things out independently. When the woodpecker appears, it's time to take action, communicate openly with others, and pay attention to every small detail.

This bird is also considered a sign of prophecy. So when you see it repeatedly or intuitively feel its presence, this might indicate that something important is about to happen in your life. The woodpecker asks you not to rely solely on the opinions of others but instead trust your expertise and knowledge.

Like the woodpecker, you can be determined and driven towards achieving success in your pursuits. However, it's important not to become obsessed with attaining your goals but rather flow within your natural rhythm while pursuing them.

Finally, if you're feeling stagnant or stuck in doing things repetitively without any progress, the woodpecker shows up as a reminder that there may be other ways of accomplishing tasks. Follow its lead and explore new avenues for growth and excitement while remaining true to yourself.

Zebra

Zebra is a symbol of balance, community, and individuality. When you encounter zebra, it's a sign that you might see things in black and white without considering the nuances in between. Zebra encourages you to explore the gray area where discoveries can be made.

Furthermore, zebra can help you find equilibrium between your daily life and spirituality. Sometimes, your intuition may make you stand out despite your desire to blend in. In such instances, zebra offers protection from perceived dangers so that you can confidently use your clairvoyant abilities to assist others.

Although stepping away from the crowd can be daunting, zebra urges you to trust yourself and follow your path positively and helpfully. You have the potential to influence and assist many individuals on this journey toward self-discovery. Trusting yourself will set you free to run wild with absolute freedom.

Angels At A Glance

Elements: High-vibrational, loving, non-judgy.
Talents: Healing emotional issues, resolving fears, and compassion for all beings.
Traits: You're a compassionate soul who truly cares for others and can't be happy without everyone else being comfortable. You're a healer and bringer of peace.

While there are Angels beyond count, we commonly work with the most well know 15 Though non-denominational, archangels are named throughout many religions and spiritual practices worldwide. They are neither male nor female but hold more traditionally masculine or feminine energetic qualities and are sometimes referred to as "he" or "she." However, this distinction does not matter to the Archangels; therefore, call them whatever feels right to you.

Remember, it's about energy, not a physical body or attribute. The Archangels desire to create peace and love. They were created specifically to assist humans with their journey on Earth. Call on the Archangels when you feel afraid or unsure. They will bless you with what you need. Take the time to thank the Archangels for all the love and light they create in your life.

Ariel
Azrael
Chamuel
Gabriel
Haniel
Jeremiel
Jophiel
Metatron
Michael
Raguel
Raphael
Raziel
Sandalphon
Uriel
Zadkiel

Runes

The Germanic tribes of Northern Europe used runes for religious and secular purposes—the earliest examples of runes phonetically representing language date back to the second century BCE. The development of the rune alphabet was spurred by increased trade activity with Mediterranean cultures that already had a fully developed alphabet.

Before, the runes were primarily used as a magical system of pictographs representing natural forces and objects. People believed that invoking the appropriate rune could contact the corresponding force in nature.

There were several different runic alphabets throughout Northern Europe over the centuries, but the most common is the Germanic alphabet.

Tyr / Thorn
Tyr represents the powerful god of warriors, known for his determination.

Beorc / Berkana / Berkano
Beorc represents the birch tree and new beginnings.

Ehwaz / EH
Ehwaz represents the noble and powerful horse.

Man / Mannaz / Mann
Mannaz represents the concept of humanity.

Lagu / Laguz /Logr / Laf
Laguz represents the raw and untamed energy of water.

Ing / Inguz / Ingwaz
Inguz represents the god Ing and symbolizes the abundance of fertility.

Dag / Dagaz / Daeg
Daeg represents the end of one cycle and start of a new one.

Odal / Othila / Othala / Ethel
Othala represents home and family, symbolizing those around us.

Feoh / Fehu / FE / FA
Fehu, a rune that translates to "cattle," denotes abundance and fertility.

UR / Uruz
Uruz, a rune that translates to "wild ox," represents determination, courage.

Thorn / Thurisaz
Thurisaz is a complex symbol that has a few different translations..

AS / Ansur / Ansuz / OS
Ansuz symbolizes the breath of Odin and can represent the concept of a god.

Runes

 Rad / Raido / Reidh / Raidho
Raido represents the concept of a journey, both literally and spiritually.

 Ken / Kenaz / Kano
Kenaz represents the concept of a torch, which symbolizes illumination.

 Gifu / Gebo
Gifu represents the gift or exchange.

 Wyn / Wunjo / Wynn
Wunjo brings the concept of joy.

 Hagall / Hagalaz / Haegl / Hagal
Hagalaz represents hail, symbolizing the destructive power of nature.

 NYD / Nauthiz / Naudhr
Nauthiz represents necessity and the struggle that comes with it.

 IS / Isa / ISS
Isa symbolizes the concept of ice or being frozen.

 Jera / Ger
Jera signifies the idea of reaping the rewards of one's labor.

 Elhaz / Algiz / Eolh
Eihwaz is a rune that represents the ash or yew tree.

 Peorth / Perth / Perthro
Perthro represents the concept of fortune.

 Eolh / Eihwaz
Eolh represents the concept of the elk, but in the context of protection.

 Sigel / Sowelu / Sowilo
Sigel represents the life-giving energy of the sun and the illumination it brings.

Correspondence
Flowers and Herbs

These worksheets can help you organize and personalize correspondences for your Sabbat celebration. You can use them to research and document correspondences that are meaningful to you and your unique way of celebrating the Sabbat. Feel free to add other herbs and flowers to personalize your unique celebration of this Sabbat. In addition, there is a section on how to dry herbs and make an infusion oil.

The author and Publisher cannot take any responsibility for any adverse effects of using plants. Always seek advice from a professional before using a plant medicinally.

Foraging Calendar

January, February, and March
Chickweed, Common Mallow Leaves, Common Sorrel,
Cowberry, Crow Garlic, Dandelion Root, Garlic Mustard,
Ground Elder, Hairy Bittercress, Nettles, Pignut, Sheep's
Sorrel, Silver Birch Sap, Wild Garlic, Winter Cress,
and Wood Sorrel

April, May, and June
Beech Leaves, Borage, Broom, Chickweed, Cleavers,
Common Poppy, Dandelion Leaves and Roots, Dog
Rose Flowers, Elderflower, Garlic, Mustard, Ground
Elder, Hawthorn Blossom, Hops, Nettles, Pignuts,
Sheep's Sorrel, Spearmint, Sweet Cicely, Watercress,
Wild Garlic, Wild Thyme, Wood Sorrel, and Yarrow

July, August, and September
Acorns, Apples, Beech Nuts, Bilberries, Blackberries,
Burdock, Chamomile, Chickweed, Chicory, Cleavers,
Common Mallow, Dandelion Leaves and Flowers,
Elderberry, Fat Hen, Garlic, Mustard, Gooseberries,
Hawthorn Berries, Hazelnuts, Horseradish, Juniper Berries,
Nettle, Plums, Rowan Berries, Sheep's Sorrel, Spearmint,
Sweet Chestnuts, Sweet Cicely, Walnuts, Wild Cherries,
Wild Strawberries, Wild Thyme, Wood Sorrel, and Yarrow

October, November, and December
Chestnuts, Chickweed, Crab Apples, Hawthorn
Berries, Horseradish, Nettles, Rosehips, Sheep's Sorrel,
Sloes, Spearmint, Sweet Chestnuts, and Walnuts

I live in the North Eastern United States; you may find different species depending on
where you live.

Drying Herbs & Flowers

You can dry your fresh herbs and flowers using a couple of different methods:

Lay them on a towel or dry surface and use a stick to weigh them down. Use an old mesh produce bag! Place the herbs in the bag and set it in direct sunlight. Using a produce bag also allows you to flip the herbs so that they dry evenly and prevent them from blowing away.

Use two old window screens and sandwich them, or tie the end of a bunch of herbs or flowers with a piece of string and hang it in a dry place in direct sunlight. When it's hot, your herbs will dry out completely within a day or two. At dusk, bring your herbs inside to prevent them from getting damp and dewy. Then, they're ready to store when they are dry and crumble when crushed.

Bring the herbs indoors to dry if it's not hot and sunny. You can use a dehydrator on its lowest setting or an oven on its lowest temperature (170 or less). You can tie a bunch of herbs or flowers with a piece of string and hang it on a sunny window in your home. Use the old mesh produce bag again and turn the bag in a sunny window.

The trick is: DON'T dry your herbs and flowers in a cool or damp place. Unless the herbs are in direct sunlight or you're using a dehydrator or oven, I don't recommend drying them indoors, as it's easy for the herbs to mold. If your herbs or flowers mold during the drying process, do not use them! They now belong to the compost.

Storing: When your herbs are completely dried, transfer them to a jar with an airtight lid and store them in a cool place, out of direct sunlight. They will last for several months.

Use your dried herbs for tinctures, cooking, salves, balms, herbal teas, and potpourri!

Infusions

Infusion - is a general term used to describe the method of soaking plant material in a liquid to impart flavor to the medium. Infusions can be made from various ingredients: leaves, stems, seeds, barks, and berries are common. Fruits and vegetables work well, too. The liquid in your infusion, called the "menstruum," will vary with your intended use.

Water can be used to make an infusion. So, can alcohol, oil, and sweet solutions be made from sugar, honey, and glycerin? Different methods for making infusions can be used to create beverages, medicines, and flavorings.

Cold Infusions - are made by steeping the material in liquid for a long while and letting time slowly and gently do its work. The process releases fewer tannins than hot infusions, so they lack the bitter flavors that hot infusions can sometimes have. Cold infusions retain more of the taste of the infused material so that you won't lose the bright, fresh flavor of delicate herbs and fruits. Cold-brewed coffee and tea, known for their smooth flavor, are examples of cold infusions.

Hot Infusions - are made by heating your infusing medium before introducing your flavoring agents. Hot infusions release more of the plant's volatile oils, sometimes with a pleasingly bitter note from the tannins that have been unlocked as well. This is an excellent method to use when you want faster results. Hot infusions work in minutes rather than the hours or days that cold infusions can take. They are also good at releasing flavors that cold water is too gentle to unleash. Tea and coffee are common hot infusions.

Flavored Oils are often made by hot infusion. Mild flavored or neutral oil, such as organic canola or safflower oil, is gently heated until warm. Garlic or herbs are then added to the oil and allowed to steep to impart their flavors. The plant material is then strained out, and the oil is decanted for future use. The hot infusion can make scented oils from fragrant plants such as lavender, rosemary, thyme, and citrus peel.

The oil should be refrigerated and used within several weeks. Although the oil has been strained, tiny particles of food material can remain suspended in the liquid and act as a vector for contamination.

Infusions

Infused Vodka - *Never heat alcohol. The flame can quickly leap into the pot and catch on fire.* Instead, clean out a glass jar or bottle, add some flavoring agents, such as a handful of berries or the husk of a vanilla bean, and cover them with vodka. Put the container in a cool, dark place for a few days, up to a few weeks, to allow the flavor to develop, shaking or turning the container every so often to distribute the liquid. Then, strain out the solids and decant the flavored concoction back into the container. Infused vodkas made with berries, a vanilla bean, grated ginger root, or chili peppers are always a hit. You can also sub out the vodka for any liquor that is at least 80 proof, which ensures that you are infusing, not fermenting or rotting, your flavoring ingredients. And don't throw out those solids! You can blend those vodka-drenched fruits into adult beverages and desserts or use them to flavor cooked foods, where the heat of the process will burn off the alcohol.

Infused Vinegar - Uses the same method as infused vodka. However, you can use this infused vinegar to affect vinaigrettes significantly. Think strawberry vinegar in a spinach salad. Infused types of vinegar are terrifically diluted with water or seltzer (at a 1:8 ratio) to create a traditional beverage called a "shrub." Refreshing and delicious, shrubs were popular in Colonial times and are now seeing a comeback. So-called "drinking vinegar" popping up in gourmet shops is a shrub, sometimes with added sugar or fruit purees. But when you make them at home, you can see how economical they are. You will get sixty-four ounces of vinegar from a few berries infused with eight ounces of the delicious shrub.

Infused Water - Slice up anything you think would be flavorful to sip on and add to your water jug, glass, or bottle. For example, cucumbers, citrus segments (or just their peels), and chunks of melon or pineapple are all delicious.

Extracts, Tinctures, Decoctions & Tisanes

Extracts - are just highly concentrated cold infusions. Alcohol is the typical menstruum used to make extracts. Use the same method described earlier for making flavored vodka, using a high concentration of flavoring material to alcohol. For herbs, you'll want about a 1:1 ratio. For non-vegetal items such as nuts and spices, you can use less but still more than the straight infusion described earlier. For instance, instead of one vanilla bean in a 750 ml bottle of vodka for flavored liquor, you will need two or three beans in a cup of vodka. Citrus is another great extract option. Pack a pint jar half full of zest strips, cover it with a cup of vodka, and let it go. Allow your extracts to diffuse for much longer than flavored vodka or vinegar. Two to three months should do it. Strained and bottled, preferably in a dark bottle or kept in a dark place, they keep for a year or more.

Tinctures - are the strongest infusions and are often used for medicinal purposes. Dried or fresh herbs and flowers such as mint, calendula, or rosemary are infused to extract their oils and leave the plant material behind. Alcohol is also the most popular menstruum to make tinctures. The ratio of plant material to alcohol is the highest of all infusions: about 3:1 for most recipes but can be higher for some. Tinctures keep for up to five years.

Glycerine - Those sensitive to alcohol often use vegetable glycerin as their menstruum when making tinctures. Be sure to use culinary-grade glycerin and dilute it 75/25 with water. Then use 1:2 dried plant matter added to the glycerin mixture. Crush the herbs first to encourage infusion. Move to a cool dark place for four to six weeks, then strain. You can store the infused glycerin in a cool dark place for six to twelve months.

Decoctions - are like hot infusions, except that you don't just pour hot water over the plant material; you simmer it for an extended time. This method is helpful for barks, such as cinnamon, dried hard herbs, and berries, such as elderberry, and roots and rhizomes.

Fruit peel "tea" can be made by simmering apple or pear peels in hot water until fragrant; sweeten and sip on a cold winter's night. Homemade cold remedies and other home cures, such as elderberry syrup (which often calls for woody herbs, barks, and dried items), are often created by decoction.

Tisanes - Hot herbal infusions and decoctions are sometimes called "tisanes." The term is used, in part, to differentiate such beverages from teas, which technically can only be made with leaves from the Camellia sinensis plant. Herbal "teas," therefore, are tisanes and not teas unless they contain the leaves of the tea plant.

Infusion: Solar Method

Fill a mason jar with desired dried herbs or flowers.

Cover the herbs with a carrier oil (e.g., olive, grape seed, almond, or jojoba). Leave to infuse on a sunny window sill for 2-6 weeks.

Shake occasionally to agitate.

Using a very fine sieve or nylon stocking, strain the infusion, making sure to squeeze every last drop of precious oil out of the herbs and petals!

Store the oil in a cool dark place.

Infusion: Slow Cooker Method

Fill a mason jar with desired dried herbs or flowers.

Cover the herbs with a carrier oil of your choice. (e.g., olive, grape seed, almond, or jojoba).

Place the jars in the slow cooker with a tea towel lined on the bottom (this will prevent them from moving around.)

Fill the slow cooker half full with water so the mason jars are about 3/4 covered. Turn the slow cooker on low heat and leave to infuse for 10-12 hours.

Using a very fine sieve or nylon stocking, strain the infusion and squeeze every last drop of precious oil out of the herbs and petals!

Store the oil in a cool dark place.

Use your infused oils for homemade balms, salves, cooking, and lotions!

Freezing Herbs

Freezing is an excellent method to preserve herbs; you'll have fresh herbs for the whole year. You can have whatever you want, whenever you want! :-)

Directions:

Cut up your chosen herb and add 2-3 tablespoons of olive oil.

Put in blender and blend for 3- 4 minutes.

Put in freezer storage bags to use throughout the year.

Or, if you will use them soon, you can put them in an ice cube tray for later.

My daughter does this with her DIY baby food, which works great!

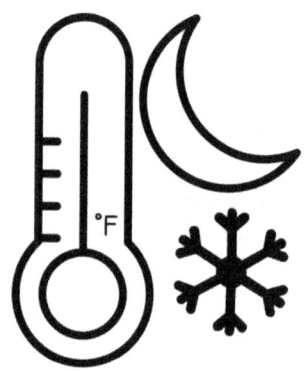

Cleansing Herbs and Resins

ROSEMARY
Peace
Soothing
Clears Negative Energy
Clarity & Memory
Boosting

CEDAR
Clears Negative Energy
Renewal
Grounding & Protection
Uplifting
Spiritual Connection

LAVENDER
Clears Negative Energy
Peace of Mind
Relaxation
Happiness
Cleansing

SWEETGRASS
Clears Negative Energy
Cleansing
Purification
Attracts Positivity
Call in Spirits & Divination

YERBA SANTA
Clears Negative Energy
Purification
Renewal
Raises Vibration
Clarity & Empowerment

JUNIPER
Clears Negative Energy
Grounding
Healing
Attracts Positive Energy

CINNAMON
Energy & Motivation
Clears Negative Energy
Healing
Grounding

Resins

DRAGONS BLOOD
Clears Negative Energy
Cleansing
Healing
Protection
Enhance Productivity

FRANKINCENSE
Protection & Purification
Spiritual Awareness
Relieves Anxiety &
Depression
Clears Negative Energy
Healing

MYRRH
Antibacterial
Clears Negative Energy
Healing
Grounding
Spiritual Connection

Please make sure the following is ethically sourced

PALO SANTO
Antibacterial & Antiviral
Clears Negative Energy
Transmutes & Raises
Vibration
Deep Healing
Cleansing

SAGE
Antibacterial & Antiviral
Cleansing
Healing
Clears Negative Energy

Acorns

Quercus Robur
Folk Name: Oaknut

Magical Properties
Strength
Protection
Wisdom
Security
Abundance
Counteracts Loneliness
Draws Good Luck
Preserves the Illusion of Youth.

Draw or Paste your herb here

Physical Properties & Essential Oil It Is/It May:
Improve Gut Health
Rich in Antioxidants
Good Source of Fiber
Aid Healthy Bones
Help to Control Blood Sugar
Provide Energy
Good for the Metabolism
Good for the Skin

Use Caution: Acorns contain a high level of tannins, which can make them bitter and unpalatable. Additionally, acorns must be processed before they can be consumed, as they contain a small amount of hydrocyanic acid which can be toxic in large quantities.

Incorporating herbal remedies into my spiritual practices helps me to grow and transform on a deeper level.

Acorn Magic

The acorn (or oak nut)is the nut of the oak tree and its close relatives.

Between midsummer and through autumn, a dried acorn worn as an amulet around the neck brings a youthful glow, good luck, and protection. If gathered on a full, they are said to attract Fairies, welcoming enchantment throughout the following month. They promote wisdom and prosperity if placed near a window; acorns banish illness and loneliness when carried in a pocket.

Acorns are symbols of security, abundance, and luck. They can protect homes from lightning and draw money when placed on windowsills during a full moon. Planting one under the light of the moon can bring prosperity to you and your home. Acorns are associated with new life, fertility, strength, and protection. They can also be used in charms to bring back lost love or ward off illness. Label two acorn caps with your and your crush's names, then float them in the water to determine if you're meant to be.

Acorns pair well with rose quartz, carnelian, and jasper
Carry an acorn to banish loneliness
Wear as an amulet around your neck for protection
Place in your window to attract prosperity & luck
Put it in your car to ward off getting lost
Pick up the first acorn you find in autumn and carry it in your purse or pocket all through fall and winter.
It will protect you from negativity, prosperity, and good luck through the dark months.
Then come spring, return it to nature as a "thank you" for all its assistance.

Allspice
Pimenta dioica

Folk Names: Jamaica Pepper, Myrtle Pepper, Pimenta, and Pimento

Magical Properties
Draws Luck and Money
Prosperity
Increase Virility
Relieve Mental Tension
Create a Sense of Peace and Quiet
Increase Determination

Draw or Paste your herb here

Physical Properties & Essential Oil It Is/It May:
Boost the Immune System
Aid Digestion
Support Healthy Heart Function
Improve Blood Circulation
Relieve Cramps and Spasms
Relieve Insomnia
Reduce Inflammation
Help with Weight Management
Reduce Gas and Bloating
Manage Blood Sugar Levels

Use Caution:

Herbal magic brings balance and harmony into my life.

Allspice Enchantment

Ingredients:
1 tablespoon of ground allspice
1 white candle
A small bowl
A wooden spoon or wand

Directions:
To perform the spell, finding a quiet and peaceful environment where you won't be disturbed is best.

Place the white candle in front of you and light it, allowing its gentle flicker to shine.

Grab a small bowl and pour a tablespoon of ground allspice into it.

Close your eyes, take a deep breath, and concentrate your energy on the spell's intentions.

Using a wooden spoon or wand, gently stir the allspice in a clockwise motion three times while reciting the following incantation:

"By allspice's fragrant power,
I summon magic, pure, and shower.
A blend of fire, earth, and air,
Grant my wish with loving care."

Infuse the allspice with your desired outcome by vividly visualizing your protection, abundance, or love.

Form a small circle by sprinkling a pinch of the allspice around the candle.

Focus on your desired outcome as you let the candle burn down entirely.

After the candle has burned out, collect the remaining allspice from the bowl and store it in a small container or pouch.

Carry a pinch of the magic allspice with you, or use it in your rituals whenever you need an extra magic boost.

Basil

Ocimum basilicum
Folk Names: Albahaca, American Dittany, "Our Herb," St. Joseph's Wort, Sweet Basil, and Witches Herb

Magical Properties
Bring wealth
Luck
Prosperity
Abundance
Harmony
Divination
Success
Peace
Courage
Strength
Stress
Purification
Happiness
Love
Travel

Draw or Paste your herb here

Physical Properties & Essential Oil Use Caution:
It Is/It May:
Treat snakebites
Help inflammation
Help to Reduce High Blood Sugar
Help to Reduce High Blood Pressure, albeit very briefly
Help to Relieve Anxiety and Stress
May Prevent Memory Loss Caused by Aging
Increase your Ability to Think and Reason

I connect deeply with the wisdom and magic of plants.

Bay

Laurus nobilis

Folk Names: Daphne, Bair, Bay Laurel, Grecian Laurel, Laurel, Laurier Sauce, Noble Laurel, Roman Laurel, and Sweet Bay

Magical Properties

Protector of Homes
Attract Prosperity
Ward off Negative Energies
Enhance Intuition
Psychic Abilities
Dreams
Amplify your Intentions

Physical Properties & Essential Oil   Use Caution:
It Is/It May:

Relieve Gastrointestinal Discomfort
Relieve Diarrhea
Regulate Amenorrhea
Act as a Stimulant
Act as a Diuretic

I manifest abundance and growth with the aid of herbal allies.

Bay Leaf - Mystical Revelation

Ingredients:
3 dried bay leaves
1 white or green candle
A small cauldron or heat-resistant bowl
Matches or a lighter
A pen or marker

Instructions:
Find a peaceful and quiet space to perform the spell without interruptions.

Illuminate your surroundings with the gentle flame of a white or green candle placed in front of you.

Close your eyes, take the dried bay leaves in your hands, and take a few deep breaths to center yourself and connect with the energy around you.

Using a pen or marker, write a specific question or area of your life on which you seek guidance or clarity on each of the three bay leaves. Ensure that your wording is precise and concise. Then, hold the first bay leaf between your palms and recite the following incantation:

"Ancient powers of the sacred bay,
I seek guidance on this fateful day.
Unveil the truth that lies concealed,
Let secrets and wisdom be revealed."

To start, place the first bay leaf in a heat-resistant bowl or cauldron and set it on fire until it burns completely. While it burns, visualize your question being released into the universe, calling forth divine insight and answers.

Repeat this process with the remaining two bay leaves, reciting the same incantation and focusing your intent on the specific aspects of your question.

Once all three bay leaves have burned, gaze into the flame of the candle and allow your mind to open to any intuitive messages or insights that may emerge.

Take some time to reflect on the energy and sensations you feel. You might want to keep a journal nearby to record any thoughts, symbols, or impressions that arise.

Finally, express gratitude for the guidance you have received and blow out the candle, concluding the spell.

Bilberry

Vaccinium myrtillus

Folk Names: Blaeberry, Whortleberry, Whimberry, Wineberry, Wineberry, Star Berries, and Whinberry

Magical Properties

Bilberries and Blueberries are a Traditional Addition to Lughnasadh Festivities all Around the World.
Protection
Protect from Negative Energy
Prosperity
Luck

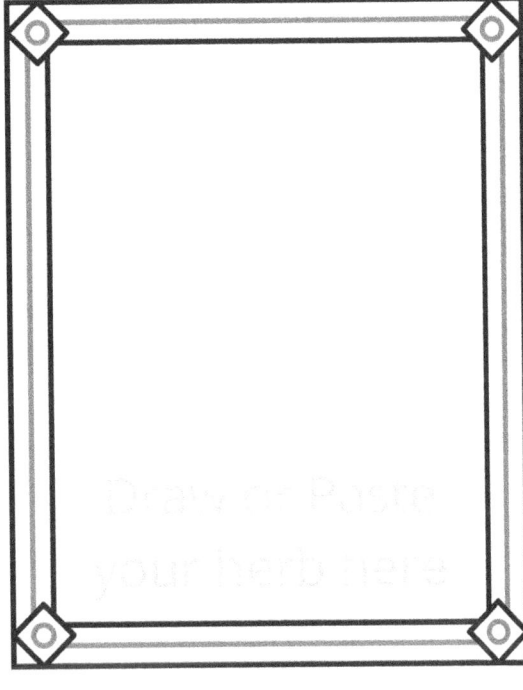

Physical Properties & Essential Oil   Use Caution:
It Is/It May:
Fight Inflammation
Improve Heart Health
Prevent Diabetes
Reduce the Risk of Cancer
Improve Brain Function
Kill Bacteria

Herbal remedies nourish and heal my mind, body, and spirit.

Bilberry

Suggested uses:

Bilberries are often associated with magical and metaphysical properties due to their rich history in folklore and traditional beliefs. Here are some suggested magical or metaphysical uses of bilberry.

Intuition Enhancement: Consuming bilberries or using bilberry extracts enhances intuition and psychic abilities. It is thought to heighten your senses and open your perception to subtle energies and intuitive insights.

Divination Aid: Place a few dried bilberry leaves in a divination pouch or scatter them on your divination space before performing tarot readings, scrying, or any other form of divination. The presence of bilberry is said to enhance your connection to the spiritual realm and facilitate clearer messages and interpretations.

Protection and Warding: Carry a small pouch of dried bilberry leaves or wear a piece of jewelry containing a bilberry charm to protect against negative energies, ill wishes, and psychic attacks. The bilberry is believed to create a shield of energetic protection around the bearer.

Healing and Health: In magical practices, bilberries are often associated with healing and promoting good health. Consider incorporating bilberry leaves or extracts into rituals or spells aimed at physical or emotional healing, vitality, and overall well-being.

Dreamwork and Lucid Dreaming: Place a few dried bilberry leaves under your pillow or brew bilberry tea before sleep to enhance dream recall, encourage vivid dreams, and facilitate lucid dreaming. It is believed to promote a deeper connection with the dream realm and aid in receiving messages and insights during the dream state.

Love and Attraction: Use bilberry in love spells, charms, or rituals to attract love, enhance existing relationships, and deepen emotional connections. Its associations with the heart and intuition make it a suitable ingredient for heart matters.

Prosperity and Abundance: Utilize bilberry in abundance and prosperity rituals to attract wealth, success, and opportunities. The fruit's deep blue color is often associated with abundance and the flow of positive energies.

Blackberry

Rubus
Folk Names: Bly, Bramble, Bramble Berry, and Brummel

Magical Properties
Protection
Prosperity
Abundance
Nourishing
Soothing
Symbolizes Life
Pagan Fairy Fruit
Attract Wealth (leaves)

Draw or Paste your herb here

Physical Properties & Essential Oil   Use Caution:
It Is/It May:
Help Stop Bleeding (leaves)
Treat bowel Problems
Improve Brain Health
Treat Sore Throats

I am in harmony with nature, embracing the power of herbal magic.

Blackberry Recipe

Blackberries are used for protection, prosperity, and energy work to promote strength and courage in challenging circumstances.

Blackberry Magic Sangria

Ingredients:
1 cup of blackberries
1 cup of sliced black grapes
2 medium sliced black plums into wedges
2 cups of cran-grape juice
1/4 cup of brandy
1/3 cup of raspberry liqueur
750 milliliters of red wine, Rosé or Pinot Noir
2 tablespoons of powdered sugar, optional, to taste

Directions:
Mix blackberries, sliced black grapes, and black plums with cran-grape juice, brandy, raspberry liqueur, and red wine. Add sugar if needed. Chill for 2-4 hours and serve.

Cleavers

Galium aparine

Folk Names: Madder's Cousin, Goose Grass, and Catchweed

Magical Properties
Binding
Connecting
Relationships
Love

Draw or Paste your herb here

Physical Properties & Essential Oil   Use Caution:
It Is/It May treat:
Kidneys
Aid Fluid Balance
Aid Liver Function
Detoxification
Diuretic
Control High Blood Pressure

I release negative energies and invite herbal purification.

Cleavers' Binding Harmony

Ingredients:
Fresh or dried cleavers herb
A small bowl or cauldron
A white ribbon or string
A pen or marker
A small white candle
Matches or a lighter

Directions:
Find a serene and undisturbed space where you can perform the spell.

Light the white candle and place it in front of you, creating a soothing ambiance.

Take the cleavers herb and place it in the small bowl or cauldron.

Close your eyes, take a deep breath, and center yourself. Focus on the intention of promoting harmony and unity.

With the pen or marker, write the names or initials of those involved when you desire harmony on the white ribbon or string. You can write your own name if it's a personal harmony spell. Hold the ribbon/string between your hands and repeat the following incantation:

"Cleavers herb, a binding grace,
Bring harmony into this space.
Through ties of love and peaceful art,
Mend the bonds and heal each heart."

Pass the ribbon/string through the candle's flame while visualizing the discordant energies transforming into harmonious vibrations. Be cautious not to let the ribbon/string catch fire.

Place the ribbon/string in the bowl or cauldron to rest atop the cleavers herb.

Gently blow out the candle, symbolizing the release of the spell's energy into the universe.

Leave the ribbon/string and cleavers herb undisturbed in the bowl or cauldron until the spell's intention has manifested. Once the desired harmony is achieved, you can safely remove and dispose of the components.

Fat Hen

Chenopodium albumhas

Folk Names: Pitseed, White Goosefoot, Goosefoot, Pig weed, Wild Spinach, Lambs Quarters, Bathua, and Huauzontle

Magical Properties

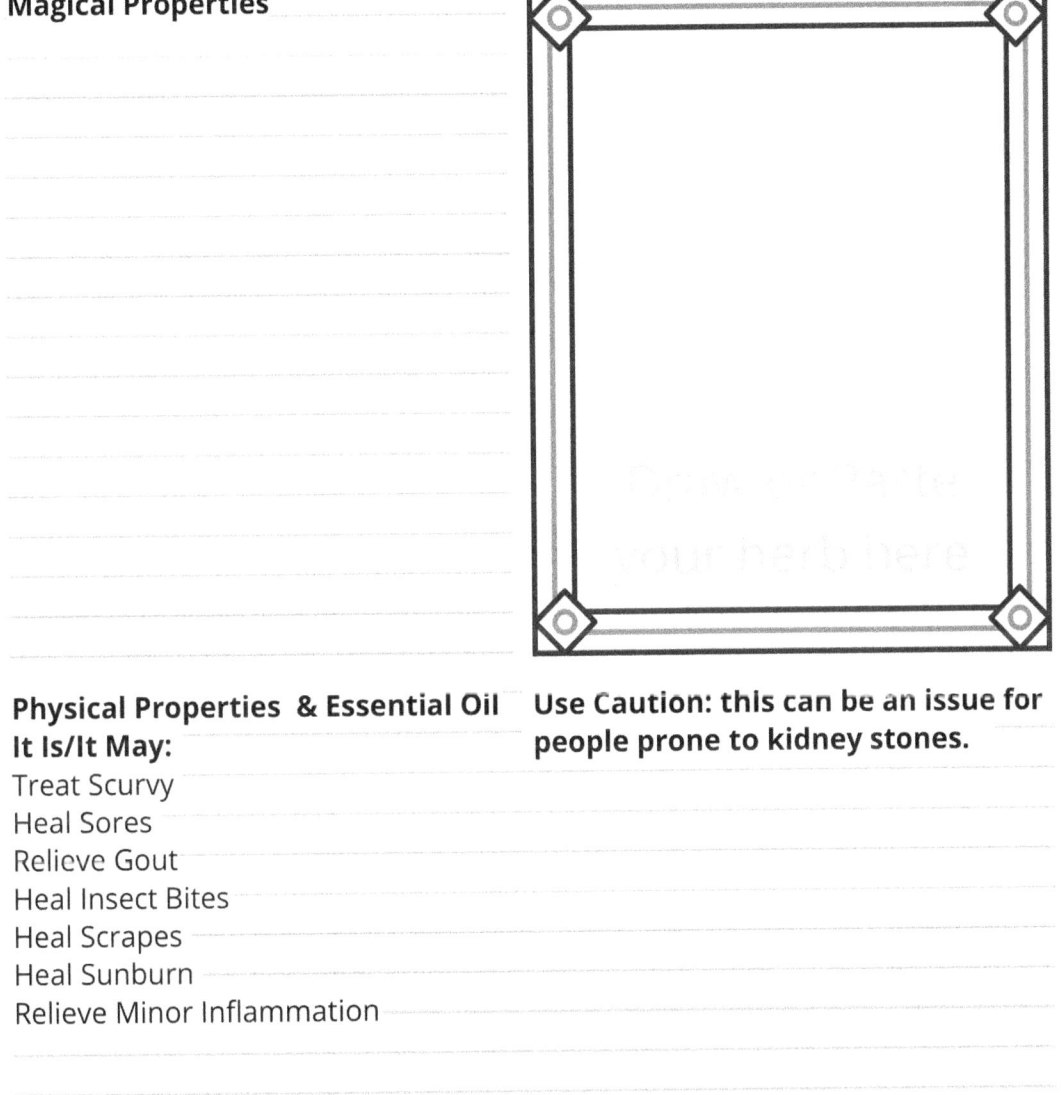

Physical Properties & Essential Oil

It Is/It May:

Treat Scurvy
Heal Sores
Relieve Gout
Heal Insect Bites
Heal Scrapes
Heal Sunburn
Relieve Minor Inflammation

Use Caution: this can be an issue for people prone to kidney stones.

I am receptive to the wisdom and direction of herbal spirits.

Fennel

Foeniculum vulgare

Folk Name:

Magical Properties

Protection Against Evil Spirits
Ward off Negative Energies
Cleanse both Physical and Spiritual
Spaces
Luck
Abundance
Attracting Prosperity and Good
Fortune
Enhance Psychic Abilities
Aid in Spiritual Communication

Draw or Paste your herb here

Physical Properties & Essential Oil It Is/It May:

Ingredient in Absinthe
High in Antioxidants
Sooth Acidic Stomachs
Appetite-suppressant
Expectorant

Use Caution:

I am attuned to the subtle energies of herbal enchantments.

Garlic

Allium sativum
Folk Names: Stinking Rose, Ajo, Poor Man's Treacle, and Stinkweed

Magical Properties
Protective
Ward off Evil Spirits
Good Luck
Protect against Infections

Draw or Tape
your herb here

Physical Properties & Essential Oil It Is/It May:
Immune-Boosting Properties
Aid Cardiovascular Health
Improve Cholesterol Levels
Detoxify Heavy Metals in the Body

Use Caution: Use caution if you are taking blood thinners

Nature's medicine flows through me, guided by herbal wisdom.

Horseradish

Armoracia rusticana
Folk Names: Mountain radish, Red cole, and Horse Plant.

Magical Properties:
Clear out Evil Power
Diffuse Spells
Aphrodisiac

Draw or Paste your herb here

Physical Properties & Essential Oil It Is/It May:
Ease Lower Back Pain
Treat TB, Coughs, Colic, and Scurvy
Lessen Inflammation
Improve Atherosclerosis

Use Caution: If you are pregnant or breast-feeding.

By embracing the power of herbal magic, I can embody a sense of wholeness and vitality.

Mustard

Brassica L.
Folk Name: Eye of Newt

Magical Properties
Protection
Faith
Good Luck
Courage
Opportunity
Confidence
Finding Motivation

Physical Properties & Essential Oil   Use Caution:
It Is/It May:
Relieve Congestion
Treat Psoriasis
Improve Digestion and Metabolism
Reduce the Risk of Cancer
Relieve Rheumatic Arthritis
Provide Essential B-Complex Vitamins
Lower Blood Pressure
Ease Menopausal Discomfort

I feel like my intuition is enhanced by the power of herbs.

Patchouli

Pogostemon cablin

Folk Name:

Magical Properties

Love

Lust

Fertility Magic

Powerful Money Attractor

Arousing the Senses

Self-Confidence

Harmonize the Body

Physical Properties & Essential Oil It Is/It May:

Act as a Stimulate

Antiseptic and Antipyretic Effects

Boost the Immune System

Relieve Inflammation

Detoxify

Eliminate Body Odor

Act as an Aphrodisiac

Promote Skin and Hair Health

Soothe Inflammation

Aid as an All-purpose Insect Repellent

Use Caution:

Herbal spells and charms enhance the power of my intentions and desires.

Patchouli Recipe

Patchouli wards of negative vibes bring stability when you are distressed and need help grounding.

Patchouli Body Spray

Ingredients:
8 oz glass spray bottle
witch hazel
essential oils (Patchouli, Orange, and Lavender)
distilled water

Directions:
12 drops of Patchouli essential oil
12 drops of Orange essential oil
6 drops of Lavender essential oil
1 tbsp of Witch Hazel (optional)
fill an 8 oz glass spray bottle the rest of the way with distilled water
put on spray top and shake to mix well
Before using this Patchouli body spray DIY recipe, shake the bottle gently.

Plums

Prunus domestica
Folk Name:

Magical Properties

Love
Spirituality
Relaxation
Passion
Longevity
Wisdom
Rebirth

Draw or Paste your herb here

Physical Properties & Essential Oil   Use Caution:
It Is/It May:

Aid the Digestive System
Help Control Obesity, Diabetes, and Related
Cardiovascular Diseases
Lower Cholesterol

I believe that herbs have the power to bless and safeguard my home, transforming it into a holy abode.

Rosemary

Folk name:

Folk Names: Dew of the Sea, Incensier, Sea Dew, and
  Guardrobe

Magical Properties

Religious Incense

Protection

Purification

All-Heal

Protection

Love and Lust

Attracts Elves

Clairvoyance, Supernormal Events

 Fidelity

Physical Properties & Essential Oil   Use Caution:
It Is/It May:

Aid Sleep

Reduce Muscle Pain

Boost the Immune System

Improve Memory

I embrace the healing properties of herbs in my daily rituals.

Rowan berries

Sorbus aucuparia

Folk Names: Sorb Apple, Witch Wiggin, Luis, Witchbane, and Witchwood

Magical Properties

Divination
Runes
Protection
Meditation
Clarity
Inspiration
Fairy Magic

Physical Properties & Essential Oil It Is/It May:

Reduce Phlegm
Boost Immunity
Combat Nausea
Promote Eye Health
Aids Skin Health

Use Caution:

I believe in the effectiveness of using herbal magic to bring my intentions to fruition.

Sweet Chestnuts

Castanea sativa

Folk Names: Jupiter's Nut, Sardian Nut, and Husked Nut

Magical Properties

Fertility

Desire

May be carried as a Charm by

Women who Wish to Conceive

Abundance

Encourage Longevity

Increase Energy

Enhance Intuition

Promote Grounding

Stability in Spiritual Practices

Physical Properties & Essential Oil   Use Caution:
It Is/It May:

Treat Severe Coughs

Help Heart Disease

Be Used as a Decoction of the Bark to Treat

Worms

I welcome the restorative influence of plants into my sacred area.

Walnuts

Juglans spp

Folk Name:

Magical Properties
Weather Working
Abundance
Insight
Healing
Focus
Wealth
Creativity
Motivation

Draw or Paste
your herb here

Physical Properties & Essential Oil   Use Caution:
It Is/It May:
Improve Heart Health
Reduce the Risk of Cancer
Improve Brain Function
Reduce Inflammation
Strengthen the Immune System
Improve Bone Health
Help to Sleep Better

Herbs are integral to my life, and I incorporate their magic into every aspect.

Herb/Flower

Folk Names:

Magical Properties

Draw or Paste
your herb here

Physical Properties & Essential Oil   Use Caution:
It Is/It May:

I feel more connected to the natural world when I incorporate herbs into my routine. Their energy helps me align with the cycles of nature.

Herb/Flower

Folk Names:

Magical Properties

Physical Properties & Essential Oil   Use Caution:
It Is/It May:

I am someone who promotes the benefits of herbal healing, and shares love and compassion with others.

Herb/Flower

Folk Names:

Magical Properties

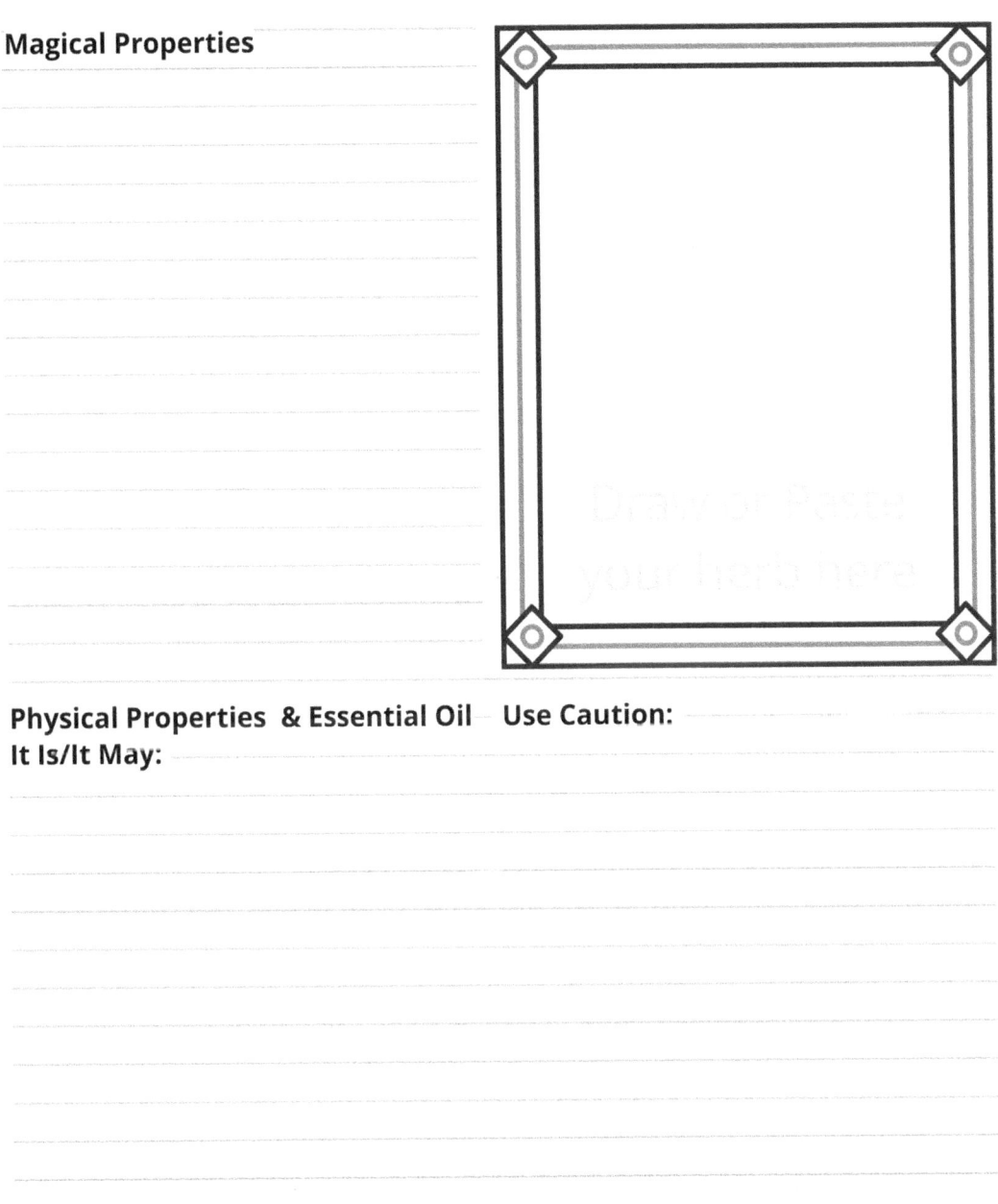

Draw or Paste
your herb here

Physical Properties & Essential Oil Use Caution:
It Is/It May:

I feel the flow of nature's wisdom as I engage in the practice of herbal magic.

Herb/Flower

Folk Names:

Magical Properties

Physical Properties & Essential Oil Use Caution:
It Is/It May:

Draw or Paste
your herb here

I hold in high esteem and show reverence towards the valuable offerings of the plant world.

Herb/Flower

Folk Names:

Magical Properties

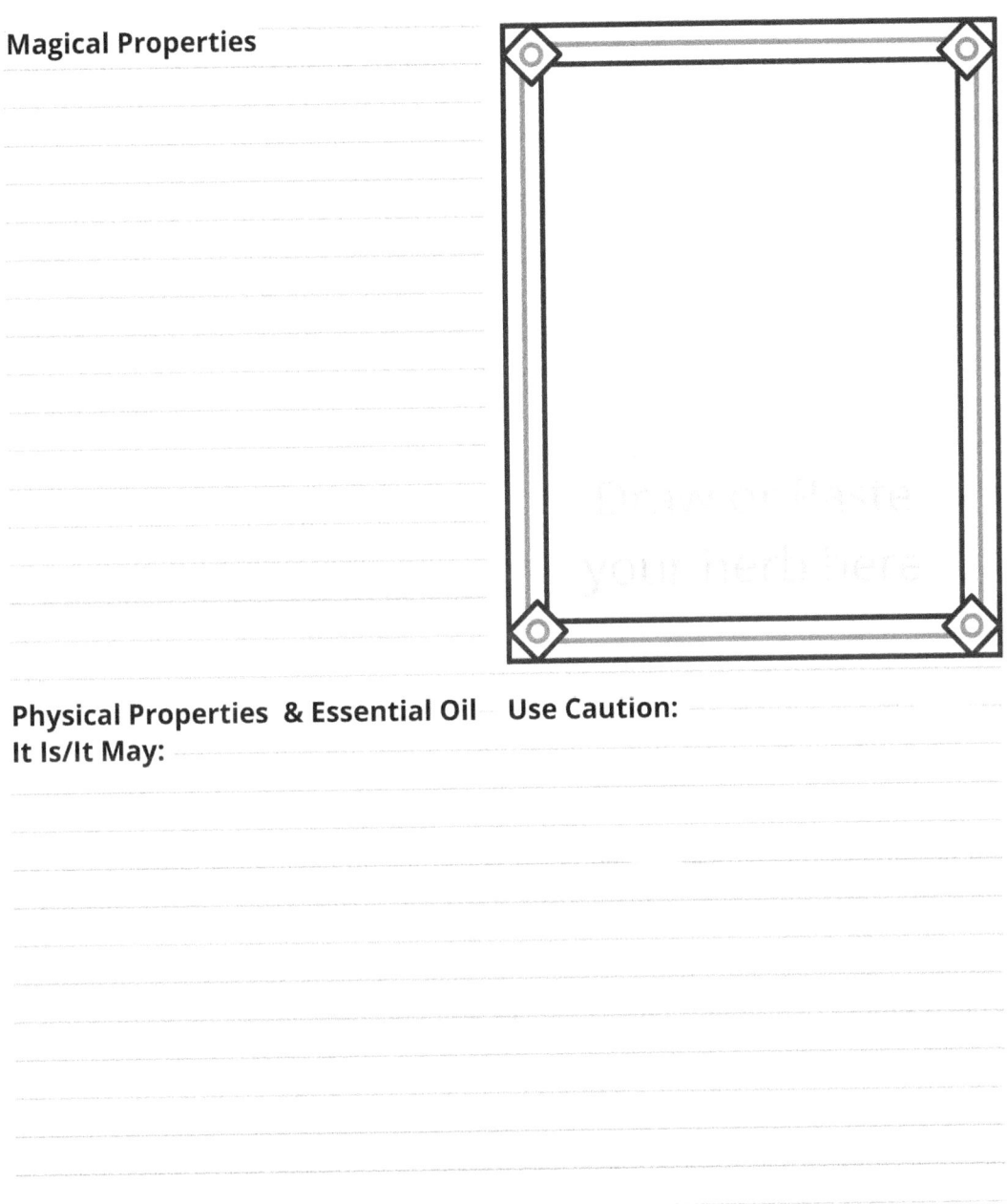

Physical Properties & Essential Oil   Use Caution:
It Is/It May:

Incorporating herbs into my routine helps to improve my overall well-being and boost my vitality.

Bee-Happy

In my last book, I talked about "Telling the Bees."

Here is a list of bee-friendly and bee-loved plants that you could add to your garden.

So plant these to help save bees:

Lavender - The fragrant plant has both pollen and nectar to feed the bees.
Catmint - It's a nectar source for pollinators, such as honeybees and hummingbirds.
Sage - Nectar from the purple flowers on sage plants makes health-boosting honey.
Cilantro - The smell of this plant causes many insects to flee from it, which = Bee safety zone.
Thyme - Thyme provides nectar and pollen and may help protect bees against disease.
Fennel - Fennel blooms in the summer months, a food source with longevity.
Borage - Borage provides lots of nectar and pollen. I mean a lot!
Crocus - Early spring crocus flowers will provide much-needed food and energy.
Aster - Asters provide bees and other important insects with a resting place.
Hollyhocks - Hollyhocks provide plenty of nectar and are loaded with pollen.
Anemone - Anemones are fantastic for bees, especially as they provide lots of pollen.
Snowdrops - are a food source for bees in late winter and early spring.
Geranium - As an early bloomer, geranium is one of the best flowers for bees.
Calendula - Calendula attracts pollinators such as butterflies and bees.
Sweet alyssum - It is a particularly good nectar plant.
Poppy - Their open petals invite bees to come dance in their stamens to collect pollen.
Sunflower - Sunflowers produce a huge amount of pollen and nectar.
Zinnia - Bees Love Zinnia.
Cleome - Cleome provides nectar to many pollinators.
Heliotrope - Fragrant purple, violet, or white flowers will attract bees.

Calendula vs Marigolds

Know the Difference

Calendula - Calendula officinalis

Physical Traits
Sticky to touch, long, round-tipped, hairy leaves

Seeds
Brown, curved, with ridges/teeth on the outside

Primary Uses/Plant Properties
Has highly desirable
herbal properties
Dye plant
Edible flowers

Marigolds - Tagetes erecta, Tagetes patula

Physical Traits
Smooth to touch, long, thin, toothed leaves and
densely packed petals.

Seeds
Straight, black, white-tipped

Primary Uses/Plant Properties
Companion planting as a pest deterrent
Dye plant

Marigold Magic

Cleansing Sticks

I've included this information now so you'll have ample time to gather marigolds for this spell later in the year for Samhain.

Smudge sticks are used in Native American cultures to purify homes. Burning sacred herbs releases smoke that attaches to negative energy and eliminates it. Smudging can promote positive and calming vibes. To avoid cultural appropriation, we will use different ingredients.

During Dia de los Muertos or Day of the Dead, the smudge stick has a couple of other purposes.

To ensure a safe return for our loved ones from the land of the dead, it is recommended to light a smudge stick a day or two before the Day of the Dead celebrations. The scent of smudge sticks can guide our departed loved ones back to us and allow us to connect with them through the sense of smell, providing an herbal connection. For a lovely offering, we can wrap dried sweetgrass with marigold flowers and secure them with red and white string.

Marigolds symbolize Dia de los Muertos and guide the departed back to us. Some see them as representing the fragility of life.

Ingredients:
Sweetgrass braid
Fresh Marigold flowers
Kitchen twine
Scissors

Directions:
To make cleansing sticks, cut sweet grass braid to desired length and trim marigolds to match. Wrap marigold stems around sweet grass and secure them with twine. Let dry for 2 weeks before burning. Lasts up to a year.

Sunflower Magic

Symbolize joy, good luck, truth, and loyalty and are associated with fertility, abundance, and the Sun.

Sunflowers are connected to the SUN.
Eat sunflower seeds to invoke joy and vitality
Infuse into oils and salves and anoint yourself to see the fairy folk
Grow sunflowers in the garden to bring good fortune to the household
Adorn wreaths, crowns, and your altar with sunflowers for Summer and Fall sabbats.

Sunflower: Asteraceae Helianthus Annuus

The Sunflower has devoted its very shape to worshiping the Sun, which gives us light and life. A living expression of sacred geometry, the golden ratio is visible in the spiraling of the Sunflower's florets.

The Victorian language of flowers gave it various connotations so that in certain contexts, it stood for lofty ideas or, less flatteringly, as a symbol for false riches.

Spirits of the dead are drawn to this flower, for it reminds them of the sunlit world they once lived within.

Faery flower sorcery sees the Sunflower as harnessing the Sun's energy, making it useful for positive magic and lightwork. The light contained in its yellow petals radiates strength, useful for dispelling depression and encouraging a healthy sense of pride.

Sunflowers
Cut a sunflower at sunset while making a wish; it will come true by the next evening as long as it is not too grand.
Sleep with a sunflower under your bed allows you to find out the truth
Sunflowers are good luck for green witches and gardeners
Plant sunflowers outside your house to repel negativity and attract courage, strength of mind, unconditional joy, and healing for emotional wounds.

Sunflower Mojo

Sunflower Psychic Protection Mojo

Ingredients:
sunflower seeds
essence and its image
a tiny light-colored bag
a very long cord
crystals: carnelian and black tourmaline
a white candle

Directions:
In the midday sun, cast a circle, sit within, light your candle, and surround yourself with your seeds, images, and essence. You are charging all these items. Focus on the Sun, the Gods of the Sun, and the power and strength of the Sunflower.

Hold your items up to the sun as you say:

"Protect me, Wildflower of Sun and Light.
Strengthen my Power with what is Right Those who send dark, your light will turn My mind; my self will now stand firm."

Close your Casting circle with thanks.
Place the seeds and crystals in the tiny bag and wear it above your Solar Plexus area.

Your essence and image are also empowered, and you may like to hang the image in your work areas.

Bay Magic

Bay Leaf Petition

Ingredients:
Dried Bay leaves
Candle
Tongs
Matches/lighter
Cauldron or a fireproof dish

Directions:
Take one or more bay leaves and a pen or marker.
Light your candle.

On your bay leaf, write down something you wish to manifest or a goal you want to achieve.

Hold the bay leaves in your hands and visualize your desires as though they have already manifested. Focus on the feeling of already having achieved your goals.
Take your bay leaf in your tongs and carefully hold it in the flame until it burns almost entirely (be careful, they can spit!).

Place it in the cauldron and watch as your desires are transformed and sent out into the universe to be manifested into reality!

Witchy Tip for bay leaves

If it crackles and burns brightly, then the outcome is positive. The outcome will be negative if the leaf refuses to burn or smokes.

If the leaf is new, it may not be easy to burn due to the moisture content. On the other hand, if it is ancient, it might not burn either.

Carry bay leaves to ward off evil.
I put them in my tarot/oracle deck pouch with a crystal.

Fruit Magic

Watermelon Magic:

Watermelon is associated with the Water element and is ruled by the Moon. The Ancient Egyptians consumed this fruit, which was highly respected for its healing properties. Eating watermelon is believed to attract love and boost fertility while drinking it in a smoothie can bring joy and peace and unblock chakras.

Cherry Magic:

Cherries are associated with Venus and Water and are believed to possess a powerful love charm. Eating them is believed to attract love into one's life. Consuming the juice before love divination rituals may reveal the names of potential future partners.

Orange Magic:

Oranges are associated with the Sun and Fire, making them a potent love enhancer in any ritual. They are also connected to the sacral chakra, encouraging creativity and promoting healthy sexuality. Eating oranges brings happiness, and placing them in stockings during Christmas is believed to usher in the Sun's return and bring good fortune to the household.

Lemon Magic:

Lemon is known to have purifying properties when combined with the Moon and Water. Adding lemon juice to your mop water can effectively rid your home of negative vibes. Adding a tablespoon of lemon juice to your bath can help cleanse your aura. To attract blessings into your home, try sticking color-headed pins into a lemon and hanging it from a window.

Pumpkin Magic:

According to folklore, pumpkins are associated with the Moon and Water and possess magical properties such as promoting prosperity, creativity, fertility, and warding off evil. During the festival of Samhain, carving a pumpkin into a Jack-o-Lantern is said to protect the home from malevolent spirits. Consuming pumpkin pie or soup is believed to bring wealth and success. Additionally, pumpkin seeds can be added to bags or bottles to attract good fortune and fertility.

Strawberry Magic:

The strawberry is associated with Venus and Water and is considered sacred to the Goddesses Freya and Berchta. It is believed that consuming strawberries can attract love towards oneself while carrying their leaves can bring good luck.

Blueberry Magic:

Blueberries have magickal associations with luck, protection, dream magick, and hex breaking. Brew a cup of blueberry tea before or after meditation to enhance the experience. To improve your memory, place a blueberry over your third eye and meditate; once done, consume the blueberry. During a full moon, dress a white candle with powdered blueberry and use it for peace rituals.

Mango Magic:

The mango fruit is known for its spiritual and happiness-inducing properties. It is believed that consuming mango can boost self-confidence, personal power, and success, as it is associated with the solar plexus. Additionally, the mango is considered a symbol of love and joy, often given as a gift to enhance the recipient's luck and as a gesture of friendship. You may also include it in rituals involving friends, especially during a full moon Esbat.

Coconut Magic:

The coconut has various magical and medicinal benefits, such as purification and protection. It is believed to possess magical properties that enhance fertility and promote chastity. Although these concepts may seem contradictory, their final outcome depends on the individual who practices them. The sturdy shell of the coconut symbolizes protection, and it can be filled with herbs, crystals, or other objects and buried on one's property to safeguard the home. Additionally, consuming coconut milk and eating coconut is believed to boost fertility and promote love.

Lime Magic:

Lime has magical associations with happiness, purification, and healing. It is often used in spells for these purposes.

Pear Magic:

Pear Magic is often associated with magic used to bring love, peace, happiness, and luck. It is commonly used in spells for these specific purposes.

Pineapple Magic:

Pineapple has magical associations with prosperity, love, and friendship and is often used in spells for these purposes.

Tomato Magic:

Did you know that tomatoes are often associated with love and prosperity? Some call them the "Love Apple" due to their aphrodisiac properties. Consider serving tomato sauce and pasta to your loved ones to enhance the loving energy in your home. And if you have a garden, growing tomatoes can help protect your space from negative influences and attract abundance.

Apple Magic:

Did you know that apples have cultural and mythological significance? They are associated with the Mother Goddess, the Isle of Avalon, and the Otherworld. You can find a five-pointed star inside if you cut an apple horizontally. Additionally, apples are believed to possess magical properties, particularly regarding love and vitality.

Grape Magic:

Grapes have been linked to fertility and the magical properties of gardens. Additionally, they are believed to enhance mental abilities and can be utilized in money spells. To draw wealth, place them on your altar or consume them before casting a money spell. Remember to use them wisely.

Raspberry Magic:

Raspberries are associated with the element of water and have a variety of properties. They are believed to embody fertility, kindness, love, patience, protection, magical potency, feminine energy, lust, feminine strength and health, imagination, youth, creativity, happiness, passion, dream magic, libido, marriage, affection, fidelity, and desire. Additionally, carrying raspberries during pregnancy is thought to provide protection and promote safer childbirth, potentially easing menstruation pain.

Blackberry Magic:

The leaves, berries, and blackberry vines have been incorporated into wealth and protection spells for ages. Even today, some Wiccans bake blackberry pies on Lughnasadh (August 2) to celebrate the harvest and poetically symbolize God's death.

Kiwi Magic:

The heart chakra is connected to these links, which join us to Mother Earth's love. The abundant seeds signify fertility, while the protective brown skin indicates protection.

Lemon Magic:

The lemon is considered sacred in moon magic and is believed to bring the energizing essence of the sun due to its vibrant yellow hue and connection to the solar plexus chakra.

Orange Magic:

In witchcraft, orange peel brings various positive outcomes, including prosperity, happiness, success, vitality, love, strength, and creativity.

Walnut Ornament

I've included this information now so you'll have ample time to gather walnuts for this craft later in the year for Yule.

Ingredients:
Whole walnuts in shells
Knife
Liquid gilding and craft paint
Paintbrushes
Twine
Scissors
Pen and paper
Glue gun and glue sticks

Directions:
Gently crack the walnut along its seam to split it in half (a table knife works fine for this).
Scoop out the walnut pieces to leave you with the two shell halves.
Brush liquid gilding or craft paint onto the exterior of each shell and let it dry. (optional)
Cut paper into thin strips and write a wish for the new year.
Roll up the message and place it into one half of the walnut shell.
Loop and knot a piece of twine and place it into the other half of the walnut shell, allowing the loop to hang out of the top
Carefully place a bead of hot glue along the edge of the shell.
Press both halves of the walnut shell together. Wipe away any excess glue.
Hang and enjoy your ornament!

Walnut Spell

For Money and Prosperity:
Try always to have a bowl of Walnuts on your table. Replace when eaten.

Take a walnut.
Crack it in half. Remove the fruit.
On a small piece of paper, write a figure of how much you wish your finances to grow (don't be greedy)
Light a green candle, and drip the wax onto the inner half.
Place the paper inside the shells and seal them.
Bury the shell into the Earth.

Correspondence Crystals

I have included worksheets to familiarize you with some correspondence associated with this season. Feel free to add others to personalize your unique way of celebrating this sabbat.

Cleansing vs. Charging

Cleansing:
Removes past energies
Item is restored to its natural state
Crystal-like quartz & selenite can cleanse other crystals/tools

Charging:
Adds purpose or intention
Programs a tool for a specific energy
Charged crystals can be used to add energy to other items

Like you need to be clean, so do your crystals

Due to their energetic nature, crystals hold onto energy patterns with which they come in contact. Therefore, when your crystals have made their way to you, they have been in many hands and places. This is why it is essential to cleanse your crystals. Crystals are effective at healing because they can pick up or absorb subtle negative energies, imbalances, and psychic debris; and remove them on your behalf. There are many ways to cleanse crystals and stones.

A few crystals never need cleansing. For example, citrine, kyanite, and selenite are self-cleaning. Clear Quartz and Carnelian cleanse other crystals.

Safe Methods

Cleansing with Water
While water is a beautiful cleanser for humans, we must be cautious when using it to cleanse our stones or crystals because it can harm delicate or soft crystals. Water works best with polished stones or hard crystals. Never use water to cleanse rough stones, soft crystals, or natural geodes. The more delicate the crystal, the more fragile the cleansing process should be.
The water method for cleansing crystals or stones is quite simple. Hold the crystal or stone under fresh water for a few seconds. Never use saltwater to cleanse crystals or stones because the salt can penetrate microscopic fissures in the surface of the crystal and cause extensive damage to the structure, and take the shine off of the stone.

Water Bath: Place the crystal in a bowl of water. Allow the stone to sit for several hours, letting the water gently pull away and absorb the accumulated energy. After this clarifying bath, let the crystal air dry and dispose of the water. Keep in mind, though, that some stones can be damaged by water.

Like you need to be clean, so do your crystals

Due to their energetic nature, crystals hold onto energy patterns with which they come in contact. Therefore, when your crystals have made their way to you, they have been in many hands and places. This is why it is essential to cleanse your crystals. Crystals are effective at healing because they can pick up or absorb subtle negative energies, imbalances, and psychic debris; and remove them on your behalf. There are many ways to cleanse crystals and stones.

A few crystals never need cleansing. For example, citrine, kyanite, and selenite are self-cleaning. Clear Quartz and Carnelian cleanse other crystals.

Safe Methods

Cleansing with Water
While water is a beautiful cleanser for humans, we must be cautious when using it to cleanse our stones or crystals because it can be harmful to delicate or soft crystals. Water works best with polished stones or hard crystals. Never use water to cleanse rough stones, soft crystals, or natural geodes. The more delicate the crystal, the more fragile the cleansing process should be.

The water method for cleansing crystals or stones is quite simple. Hold the crystal or stone under fresh water for a few seconds. Never use saltwater to cleanse crystals or stones because the salt can penetrate microscopic fissures in the surface of the crystal and cause extensive damage to the structure, as well as take the shine off of the stone.

Water Bath: Place the crystal in a bowl of water. Allow the stone to sit for several hours, letting the water gently pull away and absorb the accumulated energy. After this clarifying bath, let the crystal air dry and dispose of the water. Keep in mind, though, that some stones can be damaged by water.

Cleansing

Cleansing With Moonlight

Moonlight is a popular and safe way to cleanse any crystal type (rough or polished) since they do not come into contact with anything other than soft moonlight. Place your crystals or stones outside on a table or near a window bathed in the moonlight for a few hours. Make sure dew does not get them wet. In the morning, your crystals will be ready to go to work.

Cleansing With Sound

With reverberating sound, it can be used to cleanse crystals or stones. You can use any of a variety of instruments. I suggest a tuning fork, singing bowl, bell, chime, tingsha, or your voice chanting a prayer or mantra. Allow the sound to wash over the crystals or stones and actively visualize them, releasing all of the old energies onto the sound waves.

Cleansing With Sunlight

Sunlight is a powerful crystal and stone cleaner, but only for certain types. A few crystals and stones will fade (just like some fabrics) with continued exposure to sunlight. These sunlight-fragile crystals and stones include Ametrine, Aventurine, Apatite, Amethyst, Chrysoprase, Kunzite, Sapphire, Fluorite, Rose Quartz, and Smokey Quartz. Do not place these crystals or stones in sunlight for more than a few minutes to be safe.

Like you need a boost of energy, so do your crystals

Consider it like charging your phone; neglect it long enough, and it will die. Below are some basic techniques for charging your crystals.

Quartz Points: Place the crystal that needs charging on a flat surface and surround it with three or more quartz crystals, with the points facing inward. Quartz directs and amplifies energy, so aiming it at your stone channels positive energy into it.

Sunlight: Set your stones in direct sunlight for several hours. Some crystals can fade in prolonged sunlight, affecting their magical power. To avoid fading, shorten their time in the sun to just a few minutes.

Moonlight: The full moon is also an essential source for charging. Place your crystals outdoors or on a windowsill; even if it's a cloudy night, the moon's energy will find them and fill them with power.

Candles: Light white candles in a small circle on your magic work area, altar, or sacred space. Place your crystal in the center and light the candles.

Plants: Place the crystal at the foot of a healthy tree where it can touch the roots or bark.

Herbs: Mugwort is an herb used in witchcraft to increase psychic powers. It's often used to charge tools used in magic. You can boil a bit of dried mugwort into a tea, let it cool, and place the crystal in it for several hours. You can also keep some dried mugwort in a container and place the crystal in it, covering it completely and letting it sit for several hours. Other herbs for charging crystals include rose petals, rosemary, and sage.

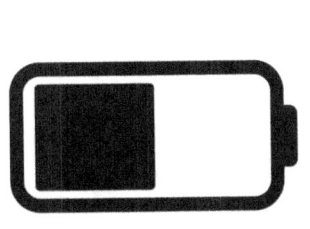

Crystals Everywhere

In your purse, pocket, or bra
In a crystal grid
In a dreamcatcher
Hang by a window or on the sill
In your garden
In a zen garden
On a necklace or bracelet
In a pot with your inside plants
In spells: sachet, bottles, candles, balls, then hang anywhere
Under your pillow
In an infused water bottle (only certain ones)
On your altar
Hang from your pet's collar
Use in your bath water (only certain ones)
Use to help with anxiety or pain

"I think I'll just buy one crystal," said no one EVER.

Crystal Shapes

Clusters
radiates unity throughout the space and charges other crystals

Pyramids
anchoring crystal and powerful for manifesting desires

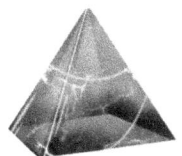

Cubes
consolidates energy, grounding & meditation, and connect to the energy of the Earth

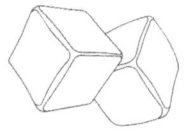

Double Terminated
absorb negative energy, grounding, break down old patterns, and promotes psychic ability

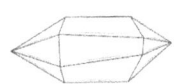

Twin
grounding & harmonizing energies, and balances yin & yang energies

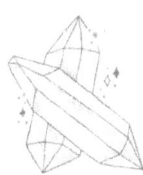

Points
concentrates & directs energy

Crystal Shapes

Wand
healing rituals,
moving &
directing energy

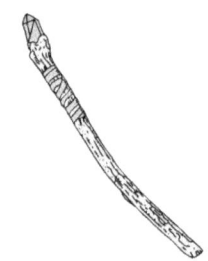

Egg
healing, fertility,
and
balance

Spheres
emits energy
equally
from all direction,
and
ideal for scrying

Druzy
charging, relaxation &
harmony, purify &
amplify body's
natural healing
properties

Geode
amplifies,
conserves &
releases energy,
and
Internal healing

Isis
feminine energy,
healing
emotional
hurt and distress

Choosing the Shape of Your Crystal

1 - Look up the energetic properties of your crystal.

2 - Consider the shape and if it offers benefits, such as enhancing any of the properties you are interested in.

3 - Consider if the crystal shape suits your chosen way of working with the stone.

Full Moon Crystal Charging: Place crystals, such as clear quartz or selenite, under the light of the full moon to cleanse and recharge their energies.

Crystal Grid Meditation: Create a sacred geometric pattern using various crystals and sit within the grid to enhance meditation and manifest specific intentions.

Crystal Elixir Ritual: Infuse purified water with the healing properties of crystals like amethyst or rose quartz by placing them in a glass container under sunlight for a few hours, then drinking the elixir to promote well-being.

Crystal Pendulum Divination: Hold a crystal pendulum, such as an amethyst or clear quartz, and use its movements to receive answers or guidance to specific questions.

Crystal Bath Ritual: Add a selection of crystals like rose quartz or blue lace agate to your bathwater to promote relaxation, self-love, or emotional healing.

Crystal Altar Dedication: Create an altar space dedicated to your spiritual practice, adorning it with various crystals that resonate with your intentions and beliefs.

Crystal Scrying: Gaze into a crystal ball, obsidian mirror, or other reflective crystal surfaces to induce visions, gain insights, or connect with the spirit world.

Crystal Chakra Balancing: Place corresponding crystals, such as amethyst for the crown chakra or citrine for the solar plexus chakra, on the body's energy centers during meditation or energy healing sessions.

Crystal Talisman Creation: Select a crystal with qualities aligned with your desired outcome, cleanse it, and carry or wear it as a personal talisman to attract or enhance specific energies.

Crystal Ritual Candle: Carve symbols or intentions onto a candle and surround it with crystals that amplify or support your desired outcome while lighting it during rituals or spells.

Crystal Dream Pillow: Fill a small fabric pouch with soothing crystals like amethyst or moonstone and place it under your pillow to enhance dream recall, lucid dreaming, or peaceful sleep.

Crystal Cleansing: Use a smudging bundle or stick to purify crystals by passing them through the smoke of herbs like sage or palo santo, cleansing them of any negative energies.

Crystal Manifestation Jar: Fill a glass jar with crystals, herbs, and intention notes, sealing it with a lid. Place the jar on your altar or in a prominent spot to amplify and manifest your desires.

Crystal Circle Casting: Create a circle with crystals, placing them in the cardinal directions or corresponding elements, to create sacred space and protect it during rituals or spellwork.

Crystal Rune Casting: Use a bag of crystal runes marked with symbols or letters to divine answers or gain insights into specific questions or situations.

Crystal Ancestor Communication: Set up a crystal grid or altar with crystals that enhance spiritual communication, like quartz or amethyst, to connect with and honor ancestors or spirit guides.

Crystal Grounding Ritual: Hold grounding stones such as black tourmaline or hematite, close your eyes, and visualize roots growing from your feet into the Earth, grounding and centering your energy.

Crystal Offering: Place a crystal or crystal-infused water on an outdoor altar or sacred space as an offering to nature spirits, deities, or any spiritual entities you honor.

Crystal Protection Grid: Arrange protective crystals, such as black tourmaline or obsidian, around your living space or bed to create a grid that shields against negative energies or psychic attacks.

Crystal Moon Ritual: During the new moon or full moon, create a ceremonial space outdoors, surrounded by crystals like moonstone or labradorite, to honor the lunar energy, set intentions, or perform divination.

Apache tears

Magical Properties
Creativity
Opportunities
Transformation
Protection
Courage
Meditation
Confidence
Knowledge
Empathy
Channeling
Grounding
Clairvoyance

Classification -
Origin - United States
Rarity -

Crystal Pairs With -
Don't Mix With -
Cost -
Got it from -
Planets - Saturn
Chakra -
Signs - Scorpio, Saggitarius
Notes:

Identification
Color(s) - Black
Transparency -
Lustre -
Crystal System - small, indented pebbles
Chemical - SiO_2

With the guidance of crystals, I attract abundance and prosperity.

Flourite

Magical Properties
Sports
Decisions
Balance
Clarifying
Protection
Grounding
Cleansing
Balancing Polarities
Life's Purpose
Mental Enhancement
Self-Discipline

Classification -
Origin - South Africa, China, Mexico, Mongolia, the United Kingdom, the United States, Canada, Tanzania, Rwanda, and Argentina
Rarity -

Draw or Paste your crystal

Crystal Pairs With - Obsidian
Don't Mix With -
Cost -
Got it from -
Planets - Mercury
Chakra - Crown, Third Eye, Throat, Heart, Solar Plexus, Sacral, and Root
Signs - Libra, Capricorn, and Pisces
Notes:

Identification
Color(s) - Blue, Green, Colorless, Purple, Black, Yellow, and Pink
Transparency -
Lustre -
Crystal System -
Chemical - CaF_2

I feel a deep connection with the universe's insights by using crystals.

Heliodor

Magical Properties
Trauma
Transformation
Strength
Stress Relief
Longevity
Spiritual Awakening
Soothing
Sense of Purpose
Selflessness
Self Discovery
Self- Healing
Self-Discipline
Resolution

Classification -
Origin - Ukraine, Sri Lanka, Namibia, Brazil, Finland, Russia, and Madagascar.
Rarity - One of the rarest beryllium silicates on Earth

Crystal Pairs With - Clear Quartz
Don't Mix With -
Cost -
Got it from -
Planets - Jupiter
Chakra - Solar Plexus
Signs - Leo
Notes:

Identification
Color(s) - Pale Brass, Pale Yellow, Green, Yellow
Transparency -
Lustre -
Crystal System -
Chemical - $Be_3Al_2(Si_6O_{18})$

My heart is filled with joy and gratitude when I experience the magic of crystals.

Magnesite

Magical Properties
New Beginnings
Motivation
Meditation
Luck and Good Fortune
Living in the Present Moment
Life Path
Leadership
Intention Enhancement
Inspiration
Insight
Growth
Expanded Awareness
Enlightenment

Classification -
Origin - Portugal, Bolivia, Australia, Chile, Sweden, France, Canada, and the USA.
Rarity -

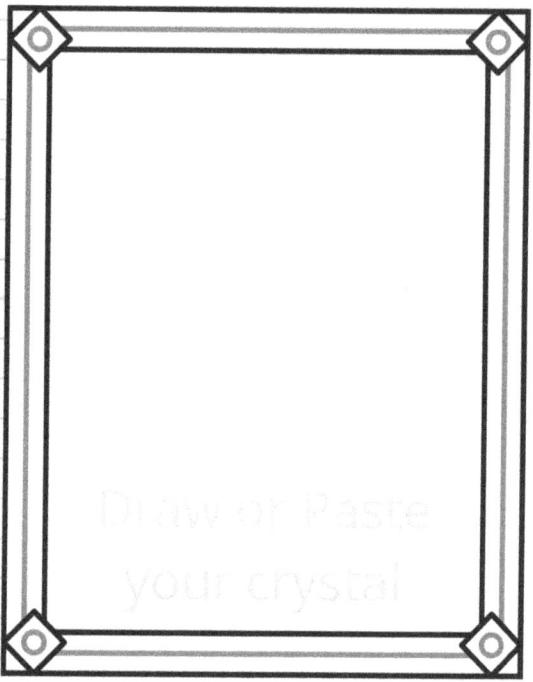

Draw or Paste your crystal

Crystal Pairs With
Don't Mix With -
Cost -
Got it from -
Planets - Earth
Chakra - Crown, Third Eye, Throat, Solar Plexus, Sacral, and Root
Signs - Aquarius, Capricorn, Aries, and Virgo
Notes:

Identification
Color(s) - Black, Brown, and Grey
Transparency -
Lustre -
Crystal System - Octahedral, and dodecahedral crystals
Chemical - $Fe^{2+}Fe^{3+}_2O_4$

I let go of negative energy and welcome the healing vibrations of crystals.

Morganite

Magical Properties
Selflessness
Nourishing and Rejuvenation
Nurturing
Passion
Peace of Mind
Physical Healing
Purification
Relaxation
Resolution
Self- Healing
New Beginnings

Classification -
Origin - Brazil, China, Australia, France, and the United States.
Rarity -

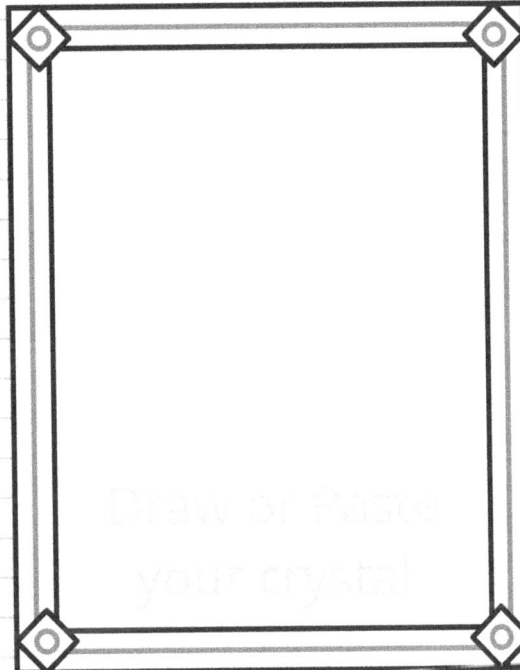

Draw or Paste your crystal

Crystal Pairs With - Rose Quartz, Green Calcite, and Pink Opal
Don't Mix With -
Cost -
Got it from -
Planets - Venus
Chakra - Heart
Signs - Libra
Notes:

Identification
Color(s) - Pink
Transparency -
Lustre -
Crystal System -
Chemical - Be3Al2(Si6O18)

I feel empowered when my thoughts and instincts are enhanced by crystals and guided by inner wisdom.

Onyx

Magical Properties
Retrograde magic
Decisiveness
Strength
Protection
Confidence
Knowledge
Clearing
Purification
Cleansing
Self-Discipline
Wisdom
Focus
Self Discovery

Classification -
Origin - Mexico, Argentina, Brazil, Australia, South Africa, Madagascar, India, and the United States.
Rarity -

Draw or Paste your crystal

Crystal Pairs With - Quartz or Selenite
Don't Mix With -
Cost -
Got it from -
Planets - Earth, Mars, and Saturn
Chakra - Third eye, Solar Plexus, and Root
Signs - Leo
Notes:

Identification
Color(s) - Black
Transparency - Opaque
Lustre -
Crystal System -
Chemical - SiO2

I feel that crystals bring a lot of love and positivity into my life.

Petalite

Magical Properties
Relaxing and calming down
Connecting with your guides
Healing the whole body, mind & spirit
Bringing magic and miracles
Boosting the immune system
Relieving stress and anxiety
Protecting from negative energy
Clearing your auric field
Releasing emotional baggage
Removing energetic cords and blocks

Classification -
Origin - Kalgoorlie, Western
Australia, Minas Gerais, Brazil,
Namibia; Manitoba, Canada, and
Zimbabwe.
Rarity -

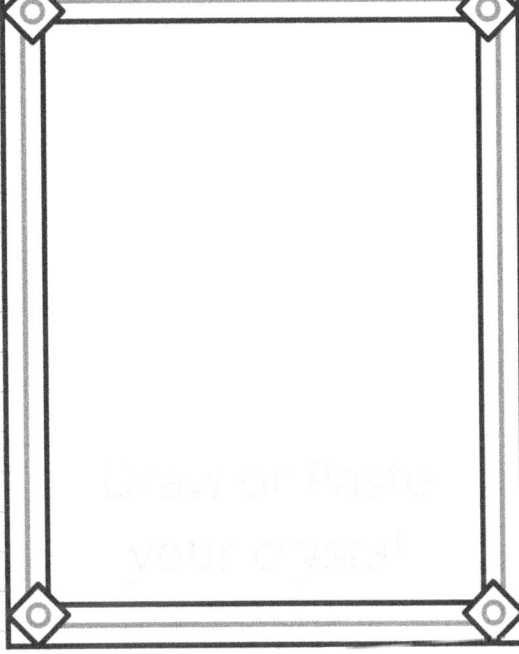

Crystal Pairs With -
Don't Mix With -
Cost -
Got it from -
Planets - Pluto
Chakra - Crown, Third eye, Heart
Signs - Leo, Pisces
Notes:

Identification
Color(s) - colorless, pink, grey, yellow,
yellow grey, to white
Transparency -
Lustre -
Crystal System -
Chemical - LiAlSi4O10,

I find that my crystals have the ability to cleanse, renew, and uplift my spirit.

Picasso Jasper

Magical Properties
Creativity,
Digestive System,
Endocrine System,
Enthusiasm,
Eye Health,
Grounding, Mental Clarity,
Metabolism, Neurological
Protection, Recovery,
Relationships,
Spirits, Spiritual Realms,
Stress,
Transition, Weight Loss

Classification -
Origin - Huánuco, Peru
Rarity -

Draw or Paste
your crystal

Crystal Pairs With - Barite, Mangano
Calcite, Pyrite, and Rhodonite.
Don't Mix With -
Cost -
Got it from -
Planets - Mars, Venus
Chakra - Root, Sacral, and Heart
Signs - Taurus and Leo
Notes:

Identification
Color(s) -
Transparency -
Lustre -
Crystal System -
Chemical - SiO2

I feel a flow of spiritual energy within me, guided by the power of crystals.

Ruby Fuschite

Magical Properties
Psychic Abilities
Strength
Love & Relationships
Creativity
Transformation
Trauma
Passion
Determination
Self- Healing
Compassion
Motivation
Self Discovery
Emotional Understanding

Classification -
Origin - Southern India
Rarity -

Crystal Pairs With - Moldavite
Don't Mix With -
Cost -
Got it from -
Planets - Mars and Mercury
Chakra - Heart and Root
Signs - Cancer, Leo, Scorpio,
Sagittarius, Aquarius
Notes:

Identification
Color(s) - Green, Olive Green,
Venusian-Green, Red, Blood Red
Transparency -
Lustre -
Crystal System -
Chemical - n{K(Al, Cr)3Si3O10(OH)2}
p{Al2O3}

I serve as a conduit for the powerful energies of crystals, facilitating the process of healing.

Ruby Zoisite

Magical Properties
Psychic Abilities
Joy
Creativity
Transformation
Courage
Confidence
Grounding
Leadership
Expansion
Manifestation
Determination
Expanded Awareness
Self- Healing

Classification -
Origin - Tanzania
Rarity -

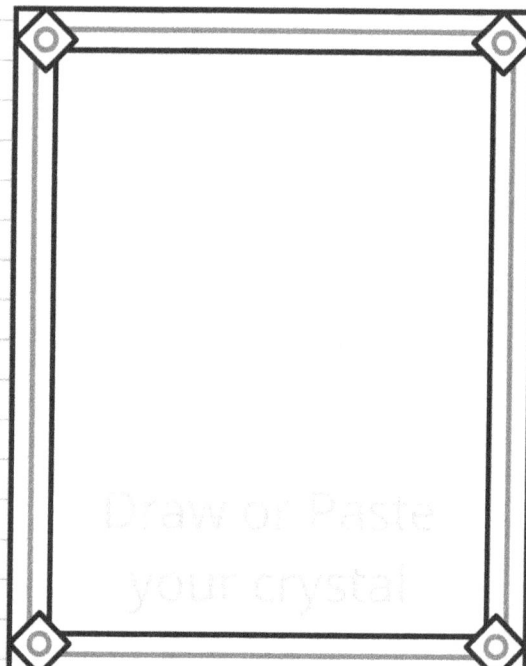
Draw or Paste your crystal

Crystal Pairs With -
Don't Mix With -
Cost -
Got it from -
Planets - Venus
Chakra - Crown, Third Eye, Heart Root
Signs - Aries, Aquarius
Notes:

Identification
Color(s) - Green, Red, Venusian-Green, Blood Red, Olive Green
Transparency -
Lustre -
Crystal System -
Chemical - [Ca2][Al,Cr3](Si2O7) (SiO4)O(OH)

I use crystals to align my chakras and bring back balance and harmony into my life.

Snowflake Obsidian

Magical Properties
Psychic Abilities
Balance
Intuition
Communication
Past Lives
Channeling
Grounding
Purification
Wisdom
Expansion
Angelic Communication
Gentle Self-Expression

Classification -
Origin - North and South America, Africa and Asia
Rarity -

Crystal Pairs With - Amethyst and Petrified Wood
Don't Mix With -
Cost -
Got it from -
Planets - Earth
Chakra - Root and Third eye
Signs - Virgo
Notes:

Identification
Color(s) - Black and white
Transparency -
Lustre -
Crystal System -
Chemical - SiO2

My crystals amplify positive energy within and around me.

Topaz

Magical Properties
Relaxation
Inner Peace
Inner Vision
Interdimensional Communication
Intuition
Living in the Present Moment
Mental Enhancement
Psychic Abilities
PTSD
Resolution
Self-Discipline
Self- Healing
Self Discovery

Classification -
Origin - Brazil and Zimbabwe
Rarity -

Draw or Paste
your crystal

Crystal Pairs With -
Don't Mix With -
Cost -
Got it from -
Planets - Mercury
Chakra - Third Eye and Throat
Signs - Saggitarius
Notes:

Identification
Color(s) - Blue, Light blue
Transparency -
Lustre -
Crystal System - Vertical hexagonal crystals
Chemical - Al2(SiO4)(F, OH)2

I use the power of crystal energy and intention to bring my dreams to fruition.

Crystal Name

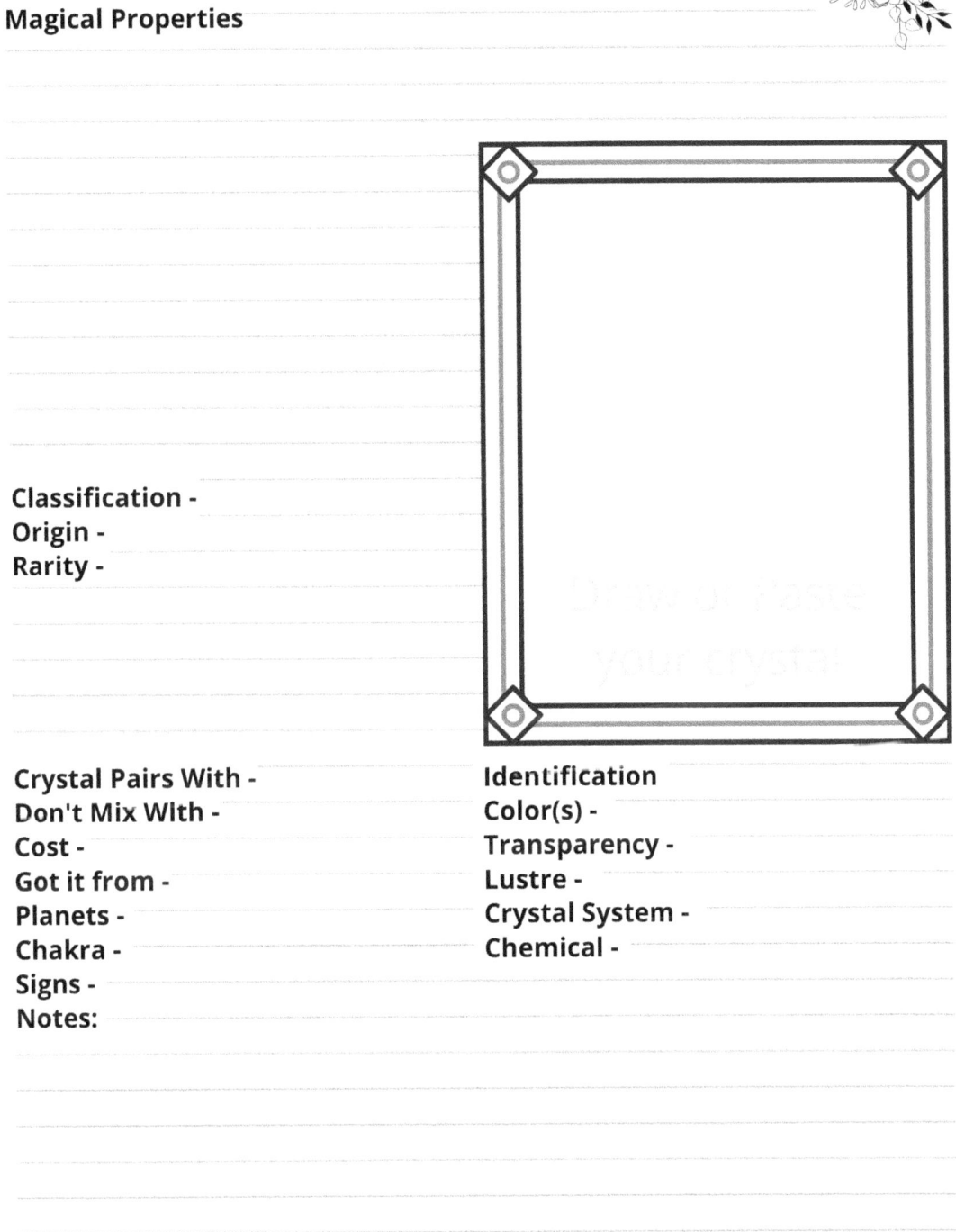

Magical Properties

Classification -
Origin -
Rarity -

Draw or Paste your crystal

Crystal Pairs With -
Don't Mix WIth -
Cost -
Got it from -
Planets -
Chakra -
Signs -
Notes:

Identification
Color(s) -
Transparency -
Lustre -
Crystal System -
Chemical -

I find crystals to be valuable companions on my quest for spiritual growth.

Crystal Name

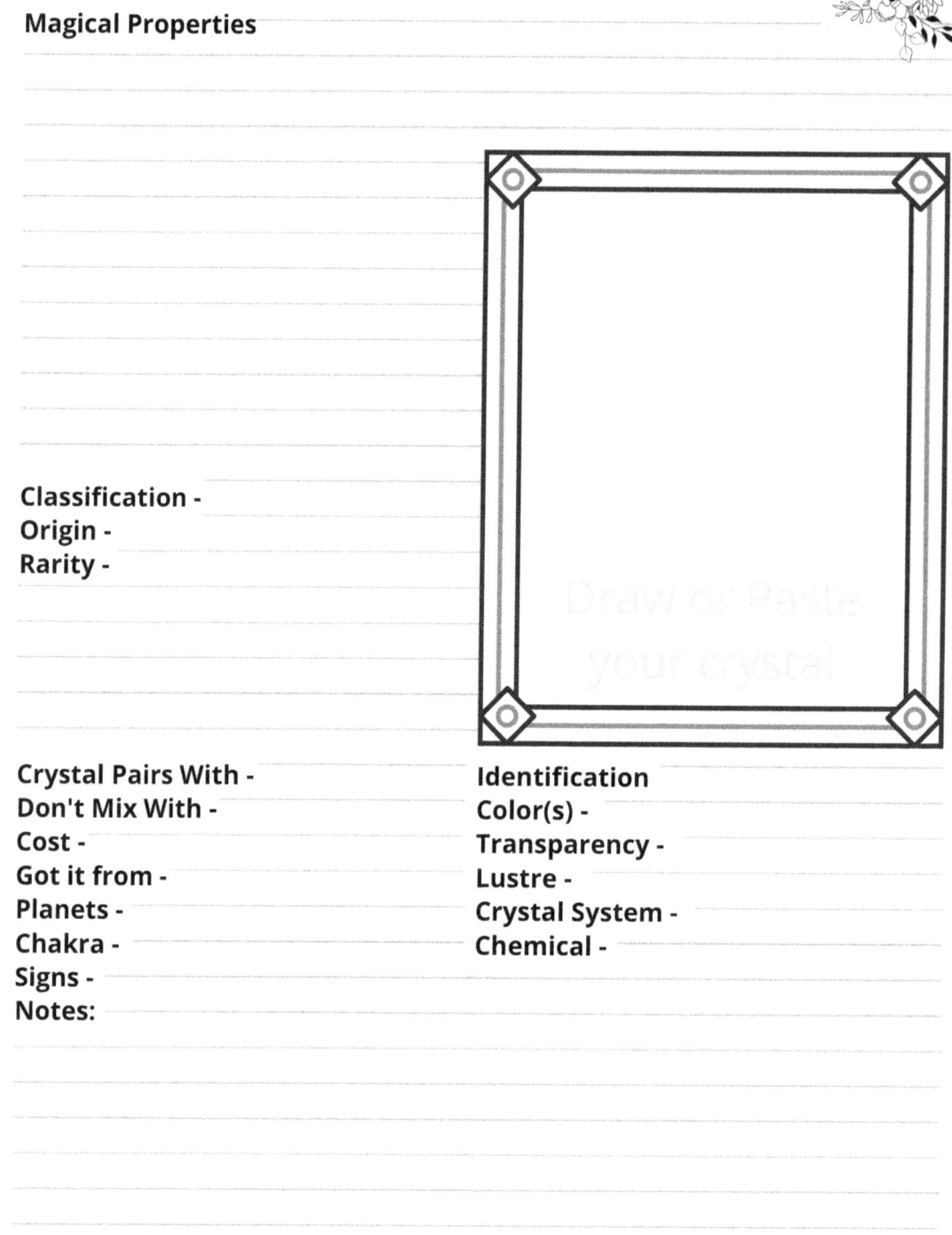

Magical Properties

Classification -
Origin -
Rarity -

Draw or Paste
your crystal

Crystal Pairs With -
Don't Mix With -
Cost -
Got it from -
Planets -
Chakra -
Signs -
Notes:

Identification
Color(s) -
Transparency -
Lustre -
Crystal System -
Chemical -

I have a deep connection with my crystals, creating a sacred bond between us.

Crystal Name

Magical Properties

Classification -
Origin -
Rarity -

Draw or Paste
your crystal

Crystal Pairs With -
Don't Mix With -
Cost -
Got it from -
Planets -
Chakra -
Signs -
Notes:

Identification
Color(s) -
Transparency -
Lustre -
Crystal System -
Chemical -

I fully embrace the power of crystal magic and allow it to help me connect with my genuine and authentic self.

Crystal Name

Magical Properties

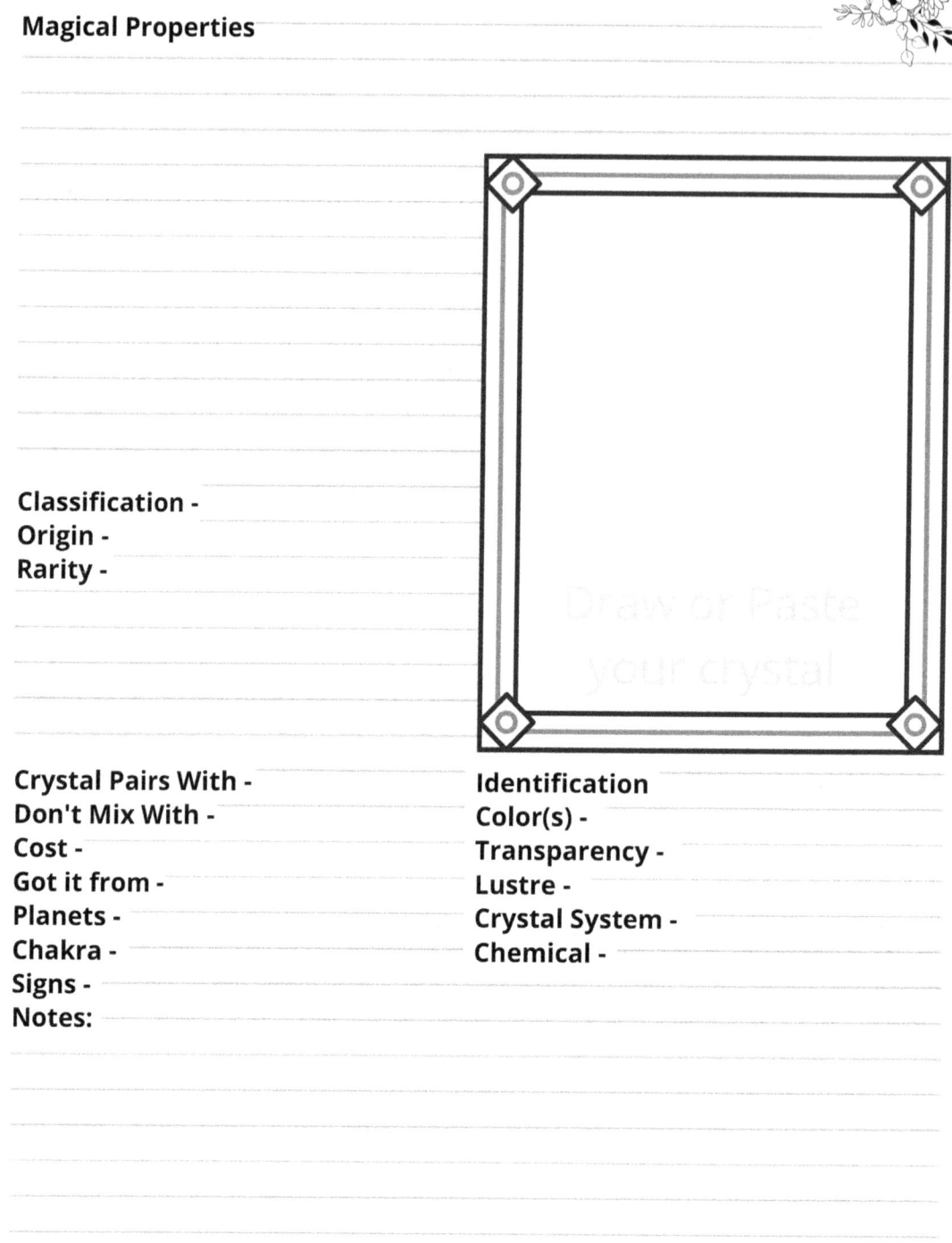

Draw or Paste your crystal

Classification -
Origin -
Rarity -

Crystal Pairs With -
Don't Mix With -
Cost -
Got it from -
Planets -
Chakra -
Signs -
Notes:

Identification
Color(s) -
Transparency -
Lustre -
Crystal System -
Chemical -

I find that crystals have the power to enhance my intentions and make them more likely to come true.

Crystal Name

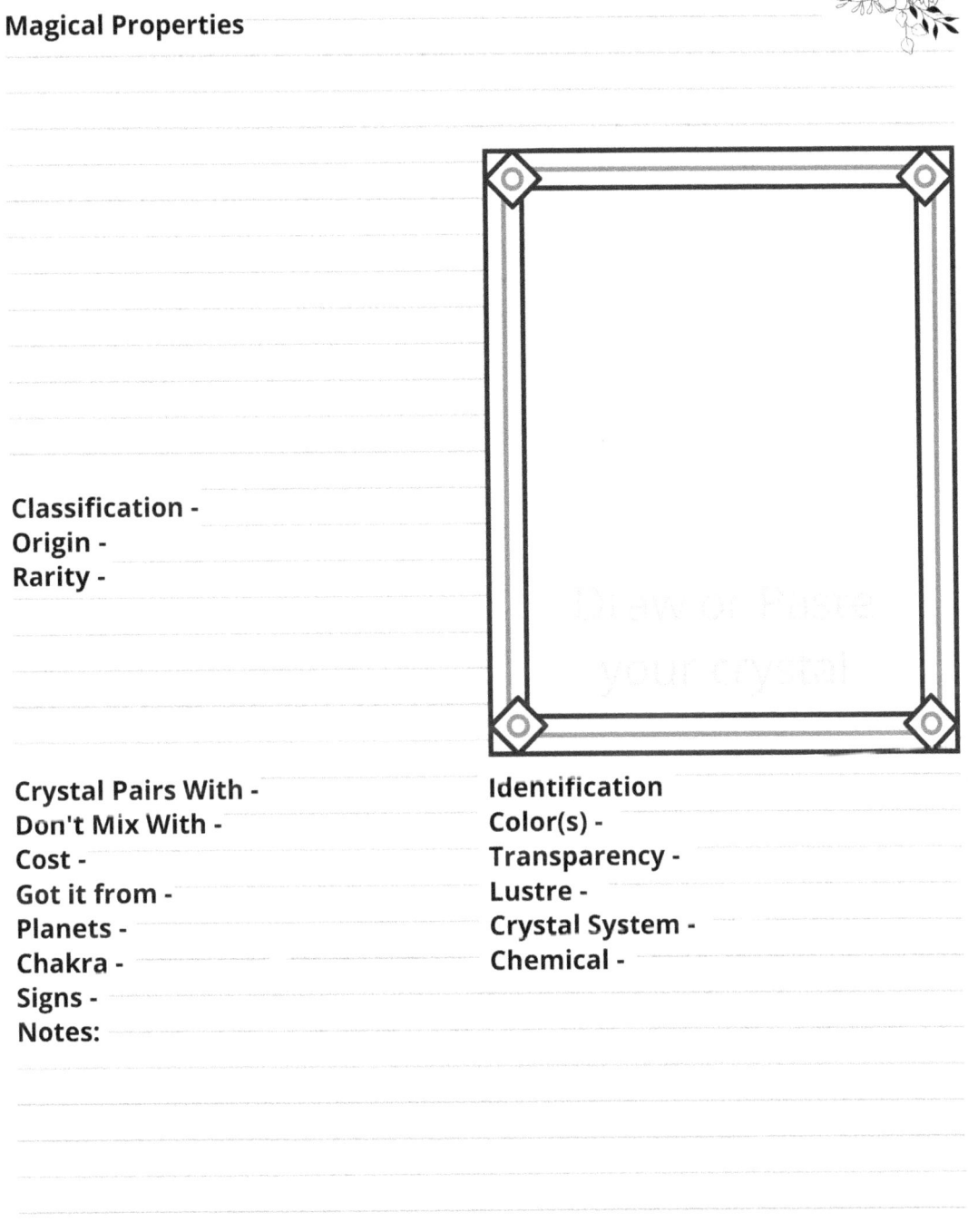

Magical Properties

Classification -
Origin -
Rarity -

Draw or Paste
your crystal

Crystal Pairs With -
Don't Mix With -
Cost -
Got it from -
Planets -
Chakra -
Signs -
Notes:

Identification
Color(s) -
Transparency -
Lustre -
Crystal System -
Chemical -

I find harmony by walking in alignment with my purpose while incorporating the energy of crystals.

If you're looking for a way to add beauty and tranquility to your home, are in the "broom closet," and need something that doesn't scream: "Look At Me, I Am A Witch," then consider making crystal bowls. They're pretty and can be used for spells and other magical purposes.

Grab and Go Combos

Insight
rosemary, lemongrass, nutmeg, orange, aquamarine, howlite or clear citrine.

Wisdom
parsley, thyme, chamomile, cumin, yellow quartz or lapis lazuli

Money
ginger, patchouli, dill, spearmint, gold, malachite, moss agate or pearl

Peace
cumin, lavender, violet, marjoram, amazonite, blue lace agate or silver

Relations
pansy, rose, valerian, moss agate, peridot or sapphire

Love
vanilla, apple, clove, lavender, rose, amber, calcite, moonstone or rose quartz

Banishing
clove, dragon's blood, garlic, hot pepper, obsidian, jet or smoky quartz

Protection
angelica, frankincense, sandalwood, amber, carnelian, citrine or petrified wood

Travel
dill, caraway, fennel mustard, malachite, moonstone or tiger's eye

Communication
mint, turquoise, tiger's eye, and sodalite

Success
rosemary, saffron, bay, pyrite, clear quartz, and selenite

Courage
horseradish, basil, chives, nettle, pepper, tigers eye, carnelian, and pyrite

Happiness
cinnamon, mint, thyme, lavender, rose quartz, amethyst, citrine or clear quartz

Health
cinnamon, coriander, eucalyptus, rosemary, sage, thyme, agate, amethyst, jade or sunstone

Binding
spiderwort, witch hazel, knotweed, agrimony or jet

Grab and Go Crystals

Abundance crystals
citrine
clear quartz
amazonite
pyrite
adventurine
tiger's eye

Mindfulness crystals
malachite
citrine
obsidian
turquoises
calcite
carnelian

Friendship crystals
rose quartz
lapis lazuli
emerald
carnelian
blue lace agate
unakite

Manifestation crystals
rose quartz
green jade
sodalite
citrine
selenite
amethyst

Stress Relief crystals
lepidolite
amethyst
rose quarts
fluorite
sodalite
aquamarine

**Breaking Bad
Habits crystals**
amethyst
carnelian
garnet
hematite
lepidolite
citrine

Healing crystals
clear quartz
lapis lazuli
rose quartz
amethyst
aquamarine
garnet

Happiness crystals
amazonite
amethyst
tourmaline
citrine
clear quartz
smoky quartz

Lucky crystals
pyrite
green jade
tiger's eye
citrine
labradorite
carnelian

New Start crystals
aventurine
citrine
kyanite
rutile quartz
moonstone
labradorite

Productivity crystals
tourmaline
green aventurine
pyrite
amazonite
citrine
smoky quartz

Motivation crystals
pyrite
carnelian
amethyst
bumblebee
unakite
citrine

Protection crystals
labradorite
amethyst
tourmaline
smoky quartz
obsidian
prehnite

Work crystals
tourmaline
amethyst
rose quartz
pyrite
selenite
aventurine

Grab and Go Crystals

New Home crystals
tourmaline
amethyst
rose quartz
clear quartz
sodalite
citrine

Anxiety crystals
moonstone
labradorite
rose quartz
amethyst
clear quartz
aquamarine

Love crystals
rhodonite
garnet
moonstone
sodalite
rose quartz
selenite

Letting Go crystals
rutilated quartz
fire quartz
smoky quartz
serpentine
black obsidian
rose quartz

Student crystals
amethyst
carnelian
fluorite
howlite
tiger's eye
clear quartz

Confidence crystals
citrine
carnelian
rose quartz
red jasper
orange calcite
tiger's eye

Relaxation crystals
amethyst
celestite
fluorite
tourmaline
angelite
howlite

Spirituality crystals
fluorite
white howlite
labradorite
aura quartz
blue obsidian
amethyst

Creativity crystals
carnelian
amethyst
smoky quartz
clear quartz
citrine
tiger's eye

Trauma crystals
amazonite
lepidolite
fluorite
black line jasper
rose quartz
mangano calcite

Mental Clarity crystals
amethyst
hematite
apatite
sodalite
fluorite
citrine

Animal crystals
amethyst
smoky quartz
selenite
rose quartz
carnelian
agate

Crystals for breakups
rose quartz
malachite
pyrite
septarian
rhodonite
amethyst

Communication crystals
fluorite
kyanite
amazonite
sodalite
smokey quartz
lapis lazuli

Good Sleep crystals
amethyst
clear quartz
hematite
howlite
agate
moonstone

Grab and Go Crystals

Energy crystals
clear quartz
ruby
orange calcite
amethyst
carnelian
fuorite

Plant crystals
moonstone
tourmaline
aventurine
amethyst
clear quartz
malachite

Driving crystals
amethyst
rose quartz
tourmaline
malachite
carnelian
jasper

Crystals for breakups
rose quartz
malachite
pyrite
septarian
rhodonite
amethyst

Crystals for the bath
rose quartz
carnelian
tiger's eye
citrine
amethyst
clear quartz

Crystals for bedroom
celestite
rose quartz
labradorite
selenite
smoky quartz
howlite

I put them in bowls and up high so my wiener dogs don't get into them. I usually add salt, lavender, and rose quartz to all of them. But do whatever feels right or gives you comfort. You do you, Boo!

My Favorite Pairings

I pair selenite and rosemary for protection and cleansing

I pair rose quartz with roses for love and forgiveness

I pair amethyst and chamomile for anxiety and stress relief

I pair garnet and pine for commitment and longevity

I pair black tourmaline and sage to dissolve negativity

I pair citrine with bay leaf for manifestation magic

I pair green aventurine and basil for good fortune

I pair carnelian and cinnamon to spark creativity

I pair moonstone and jasmine to harness confidence

Grab and Go List

Crystal Energy

Each stone has a range of metaphysical properties that can be used for healing emotionally, physically, and spiritually. They can also be carried for protection or to bring luck, boost healing or psychic attunement, or balance emotions.

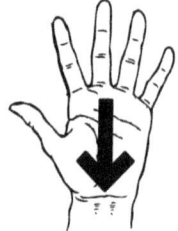

Hold the stone whose properties you want to pull out or force (project) from your life.

Example: Negativity, confusion, being ungrounded, unbalanced emotions, anger, etc. Right (Projection).

Sit quietly or meditate with these stones and focus on the energy flowing through you. Creates a continuous flow of energy (a circuit).

Hold the stone whose properties you want to bring to your life.

Example: Luck, self-love, grounding, balanced emotions, mental focus, etc. Left (Receiving).

Ring Magic

The Pinky represents the element of Air.
It improves communication, expresses your sexuality, and increases your magnetism.

The Ring represents the element of Fire.
It activates and increases creativity, improves aesthetic awareness, and shows friendliness.

The Middle represents the element of Earth.
It reduces anxiety, helps you feel more emotionally stable, and increases the desire for self-development.

The Pointer represents the element of Water.
It improves confidence, boosts self-esteem, and increases your feeling of authority.

The Thumb represents the element of Ether.
It increases will, increases your energy, and gives you comfort.

Charms Amulets Talismans

Charms
Charms are small ornaments that can be worn with almost anything and are often used to attract good luck to the wearer.

Amulets
Amulets have been worn for protection for thousands of years and are believed to possess the power to ward off negative energy, evil spirits, and illnesses.

Talismans
Talismans are objects meant to attract a specific outcome or energy to their owner. To be effective, they must be consecrated and charged with magical power by the person who prepares them. This imbues them with the specific energy required for their intended purpose.

Types of Metal

Rose Gold
Divine feminine, heart expansion, and gratitude
Silver
Moon magic, intuition, wisdom, and psychic
Iron
"as above so below," grounding, and astral travel
Gold
Sun magic, personal growth, and accomplishment
Copper
Human ingenuity, creatively and invention

Left Arm
Receive Energy
Thinking of encouraging Yin Femina Essense
Lapis Lazuli Receive peace and stimulate your power
Amethyst enhances your intuition and psychic ability
Amazonite, speak your truth and release judgment
Shungite protect yourself and feel a sense of security

Right arm
Give energy psychical action yang masculine essence
Rose quartz gives loving energy to others
Carnelian creates a stable environment for those around you
Citrine help attract wealth in your workplace
Sunstone projects joyful and light-inspiring energy

Jewelry

Left Arm Receive Energy Right Arm Gives Energy

Agate confidence
Amazonite, speak your truth, release judgment, hope, and calm
Amethyst intuition, psychic ability calming and cleansing
Black Onyx strength
Bloodstone power and immunity
Carnelian focus and stability
Citrine prosperity and wealth
Clear Quartz positivity and energy
Fluorite focus
Green Aventurine luck and prosperity
Hematite balance
Kyanite intuition
Lapis Lazuli peace, personal power, self-esteem, and focus
Lepidolite healing
Malachite protection
Morganite compassion
Obsidian grounding
Picasso Jasper will power
Red Agate success
Red Jasper grounding
Rhodonite passion
Rose Quartz self-love and love of others
Shungite, protection and security
Smoky Quartz positivity
Sunstone joy and light
Tiger's Eye luck
Turquoise happiness
White Howlite stress and anxiety

Crystal Reflections

Magical Water

Water is a revered element that holds transformative and purifying properties, making it sacred to life. In the realm of spirituality and magic, different types of magical water hold immense power and are utilized for various purposes. Each type of enchanted water has unique qualities that make it a versatile tool for spellwork, rituals, and energetic practices. Moon water offers soothing and healing properties, while holy water is potent and protective. These enchanted waters serve as conduits for intention and manifestation.

When combined with intention, visualization, and focused energy, the power of water is amplified in magic and spirituality. These different types of magical water serve as potent tools that allow practitioners to connect with the natural forces and energies around us. Whether seeking healing, protection, purification, or manifestation, the versatile uses of magical water offer a profound connection to the mystical realms.

Magical Water Properties

Rain Water: Growth and rebirth spells, cleansing, scrying, altar water, and ritual baths.

Storm Water: Vitality, self-esteem, courage, mental strength, strengthening spells, and protection.

Dew Water: Healing, beauty, eyesight, love, fertility, working with the fae, and cleansing.

Snow Water: Unthaw a situation, transformation, balance, peace, consecrating, and endings.

Moon Water: Charging, blessing or cleanse, bath rituals, powering spells, healing magic, curses, and hexes.

Sun Water: Protection, healing, clairvoyance, happiness, fertility, and creativity.

River Water: Moving on, focusing energy, warding, breakthrough, power, and charging.

Sea Water: Cleansing, banishing, protection, emotional balance, healing rituals, and manifestation.

Spring Water: Growth, holy water, cleansing, abundance, potions, and beauty.

Lake Water: Peace, joy, contentment, relaxation, self-reflection, and self-discovery.

Well, Water: Healing, wishes, intuition, manifestation, connection to otherworldly beings.

Swamp Water: Banishing, binding, hexing, cursing, and reversing.

Some recipes call for water, so why not clean, magical filtered water? For example, when putting water out for the sun or moon, use distilled water (distilled water is steam from boiling water that's been cooled and returned to its liquid state. Some people claim distilled water is the purest water you can drink.) or spring water. Then, use it in your recipes to make them more magical.

Spiritual Water Properties

Fast Luck
Brings fast luck, money luck, quick outcomes, and aids manifestation.

Love Water
Brings love and resonates with love, harmony, and compassion.

7 African Powers
Draws strength from the 7 African Orishas.

Protection
Protects you, your space, your place, and your things.

Road Opener
Removes obstacles, brings new opportunities, and opens pathways.

Peruvian FL Water
Help with spiritual work, purification, rituals, and cleansing.

Destroy Everything
Destroys all conditions, jinxes, and curses and removes all things that do not serve you.

Attraction or Come To Me
Attracts the things you want, need, or desire in your life.

Tobacco Water
Draws spirits of nature helps communication between worlds and to honor ancestors.

Success & Prosperity
Attracts success and abundance, as well as money and positivity.

Florida Water
Brings protection, spiritual cleansing, and positive vibes

Florida Water Recipe

Ingredients:
16 oz of vodka
3-5 tablespoons of floral water (orange, rose, lavender, etc.)
8 drops of Lavender EO
10 drops of Lemon EO
10 drops of Orange EO
5 drops of Bergamot EO
5 drops of Cinnamon EO
5 drops of Clove EO
3 drops of Benzoin EO
Fresh rose petals & fresh rosemary (optional)

Directions:
Add your vodka and floral water to a bowl and smell each EO before adding it to your bowl. Let your nose and spirit tell you if you should add more or less than the recipe.

Combine all ingredients in a spray bottle.

Shake well before each use.

Remove rose petals and rosemary if you wish.

Keep your customized Florida Water on hand to energetically cleanse your aura, car, home, workspace, altar, etc.

I like using it on my floors, windows, and doors. But you can use it in your bath or laundry to clean your tools and crystals or even make it into a spray.

Rosemary Water

Protection Spray

Rosemary is known for its cleansing and purifying properties. It can help to eliminate negativity and create a more positive environment.

Ingredients:
Rosemary sprigs
Salt

Directions:
Add 6 ounces (if using an 8-ounce bottle) of boiling water to the rosemary in a bowl.
Add some salt.
Allow to cool down.
Strain and fill the 8-ounce spray bottle.

Mood-Boosting Spray

Ingredients:
10-15 drops of Lavender EO
5-10 drops of Clary Sage EO
10-15 drops of Chamomile EO
3 tablespoons of Distilled Water
3 tablespoons of Witch Hazel or Grain Alcohol

Optional:
Amethyst crystals for balance, clarity, and calming
Magical Water: Distilled water that has absorbed the power from the elements
Lemon or Orange Peel in fresh or EO form or fresh herbs that you find to be mood-boosting and can cleanse negative energy.

Directions:
Add to a 4 oz spray bottle.
Shake after each use.

Spells vs. Ritual

Spells:
Powered by intention, done to bring about a specific outcome
Asking for something you want, sort of like a prayer
Almost always has a physical anchor
Less formal/structured
Done when there is a need

Rituals:
Also powered by intention
It may contain a spell but doesn't have to
Often done for a celebratory purpose
Tend to have a more structured plan to make them easier to repeat
Sometimes more formal
Often repeated yearly or monthly

Spell Types

To Banish
To Encourage
To Hide
To Cleanse
To Glamour
To Wish
To Communicate
To Sweeten
To Bind
For Protection
To Freeze
For Good Luck

Magic Flows Where Intention Goes

Cascarilla Powder Recipe

Cascarilla powder is an easy-to-make essential ingredient for protective magic. Cascarilla.
(kas-ka-ree-ah) is made of powdered eggshell and used primarily for protection and spiritual cleansing. It originates from Hoodoo and Santeria but has become popular throughout America due to its accessibility. Cascarilla powder can also help create spiritual barriers (similar to salt), add blessings, aid in protection, and is a great nutritional addition for plants in the garden!

Florida water also has protective qualities and complements the Cascarilla very well.

Tip: When you crack an egg, run the shell under the kitchen faucet to separate the membrane from the body. Removing the membrane makes a higher-quality powder.

Ingredients:
2 dozen eggshells, dried
Food processor or mortar and pestle
½ teaspoon of Florida water (see recipe)
Small glass jar/sealable container

Directions:
Bake the eggshells at 200 degrees for approximately 30 minutes to further dry them. This step allows excess moisture to cook off, making for a more delicate powder. This step is significant if you grind the shells by hand using a mortar and pestle! You might notice the color change slightly if you're using white eggshells. Don't worry - your powder will still come out white.

When the egg shells are dry, grind them into a fine powder using a mortar and pestle or food processor. Add about 1/2 teaspoon of Florida water and process until you have a fine, sand-like consistency. Store the cascarilla powder in a jar or pack it into chalk.

For Cascarilla chalk, mix 1 tablespoon of flour with 1 tablespoon of loose cascarilla powder and mix thoroughly. Add a tablespoon of warm water and mix until the ingredients have combined just enough to form a ball in your hands. Roll the mixture into sticks about 1/2 to 1 inch in diameter and let them dry for 3 to 5 days. Alternatively, you can roll the mixture into balls and place them in a small-pack paper condiment cup (the easiest method). Store the chalk in a glass, plastic, or metal container to protect it from breaking, and keep it in a cool dark place.

Note: You can enhance the magical properties of your Cascarilla powder by adding additional or specific herbs. Use caution when adding; too much of these and the mixture will not stick together and form chalk.

You can use it in spells and in making sigils and magical symbols.

Introduction to Essential Oils

Throughout the ages, natural remedies and spiritual practices have intertwined, creating a harmonious relationship that has stood the test of time. Essential oils have played a significant role in this synergy, tracing back to ancient times when they were used in magic and pagan traditions. As a result, these potent oils were recognized for their profound connection to the natural world and their ability to enhance spiritual practices.

Even in modern times, essential oils hold a significant place in witchcraft, enchanting practitioners with their diverse and magical properties. These oils offer many benefits, promoting healing, relaxation, and spiritual well-being. The essence of plants and their energetic vibrations allow practitioners to access and channel the mystical forces of the universe.

In the realm of witchcraft and other pagan rituals, essential oils are utilized for various purposes, each with its unique energetic signature. Lavender essential oil, for example, is often used in spells and rituals focused on promoting relaxation, tranquility, and restful sleep. Rose essential oil, on the other hand, is frequently used in love spells or rituals that seek to attract romance and deepen emotional connections.

By incorporating essential oils into their practice, witches, and pagans can forge a profound connection with the natural world and the energies that reside within it. They can tap into the limitless potential of nature, aligning themselves with the elemental forces and ancient wisdom.

If you want to explore the mystical world of essential oils, there are various ways to incorporate them into your practice. For example, anointing candles or ritual tools with specific oils infuses them with intention and energy. Creating personalized blends can enhance their magical properties and cater to your specific needs. Additionally, incorporating essential oils into meditation or energy work can deepen your connection with the spiritual realm.

As you embark on this journey, it is important to approach essential oils with reverence and respect. Research their properties, origins, and associations to ensure their alignment with your intentions. Experiment, trust your intuition, and allow the aromatic essence of these oils to guide you on a magical voyage where the natural and the mystical intertwine in harmony.

Oil Correspondences

For magical purposes, oils can be used to anoint various objects such as tools, candles, amulets, talismans, poppets, spell bags, and even the body. Oils can also serve as a substitute for incense and can be combined with herbs to create incense blends.

To infuse the oil with your intentions, add a few drops onto a handkerchief or cotton/wool ball and carry it with you. The fragrance will carry your intentions up into the universe, similar to the use of incense.

You can also charge the oil by focusing your energy and intentions while holding it at your third eye, by using a tool, or even by burying it in the earth. Additionally, you can expose it to starlight, moonlight, or sunlight for a brief period to enhance its magic.

Almond
Prosperity, Wisdom, Abundance, Divination, and Luck

Amber
Success, Confidence, Fertility, and Sexuality

Anise
Psychic Awareness, and Clairvoyance

Basil
Conscious, Mind, Happiness, Peace, and Attracts Money

Bay
Purification of the soul when used on the body

Bayberry
Attracts Money - Back to the home

Bergamot
Peace, Happiness - Restful Sleep and Soothes Stress

Cedarwood
Spirituality, Self-Control, Healing, and Anti-Hex

Cinnamon
Physical Energy, Clairvoyance, Good Luck, Prosperity, and Protection

Clove
Healing, Memory, Protection, and Courage

Eucalyptus
Health, Healing, and Purification

Frankincense
Spirituality, Meditation, and Astral Strength

Ginger
Energy (magical & physical) Love, Sex, Money, Confidence, and Business Success

Hyssop
Purification, Protection, and Money

Jasmine
Love, Calming, Peace, Spirituality, Sex, Sleep, and Psychic Dreaming

Carrier Oils and Their Uses

A carrier oil is used to dilutes essential oils before applying them to our bodies. Essential oils are often too potent for direct application to the skin. Instead, the oils must be diluted by mixing with an agent that will be readily absorbable by the skin, and the oils listed below are perfect for combining with essential oils. The carrier oil must be good for the skin, absorbable, and not have an overpowering aroma.

Essential oils can be applied to almost any body area once diluted with a carrier oil. However, never apply essential oils on mucus membranes, open wounds, eyeballs, genitals, inside ears, or other sensitive areas.

Experiment with your carrier oils and see which ones you like best! My general rule is to use ½ teaspoon of carrier oil per 5-8 drops of essential oil. Mix it, rub it on, and you're good to go!

I have given a particular type of carrier oil in some of the recipes, but in most of them, I leave it up to you to decide which carrier oil works best for you and your situation.

Take the same precautions with carrier oils that you would with essential oils. Read the labels to determine if it is 100 percent pure or has been cut with cheaper oil. Note the expiration dates and the ingredients, and use your eyes to determine if the oil looks clear or cloudy. Always smell your carrier oil before adding essential oil to it. Carrier oils give a bitter aroma once they have turned rancid. Ensure your carrier oil is fresh and pure before mixing it with your precious essential oils.

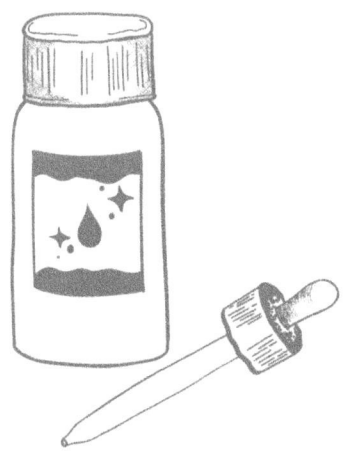

Where To Apply Your EOs

For Energy & Focus
crown of your head, back of your neck, chest, or forearms

For Respiratory Support
behind your ears, down the spine, chest, neck, and throat

For Immune Support
down the spine and bottoms of the feet

For Restful Sleep
big toe, forearms, forehead, and wrists

For Head Tension
temples, back of your neck, and around your ears

For Emotional Support
rub the oil in your hands and breathe deeply; apply over the heart and behind the ears

For Feeling Overwhelmed
lower back, back of neck, shoulders, and neck

For Digestion
1-2 drops in the belly button, and rub clockwise on the stomach

Types of Carrier Oils

Sweet Almond Oil
This carrier oil is cheap and readily available. It's also loaded with vitamins, so it's good for your skin. Almond oil will last a year on the shelf. It has lots of protein and is excellent to use in massage oils.

Apricot Kernel Oil
This carrier oil is excellent for dry, aged skin (like mine). It works wonders as a moisturizing lotion and is used in antiaging products worldwide. In addition, it's loaded with vitamin A and is a good base for healing products.

Grape Seed Oil
This carrier oil is inexpensive but has a short shelf life. However, it has vitamins A and E, so it's perfect for your skin.

Jojoba Oil
This carrier oil is my favorite and is terrific for all skin types, plus it's perfect for skin conditions. It will keep forever on the shelf and mixes beautifully with EOs. It's great for the hair, scalp, and skin.

Sesame Oil
This carrier oil works well for sensitive skin because it has protein, vitamins, and minerals, which are very good for the body and the skin.

Other Carrier Oils:
Aloe vera, Apricot, Avocado, Borage, Calendula, Coconut, Evening Primrose, Hazelnut, Macadamia, Meadowfoam, Olive, Pumpkinseed, Rosehip, Safflower, Soybean, Sunflower, Walnut, and Wheat germ.

How Different Scents Influence Our Mood

When I smell certain scents, I know it brings back memories and can totally change my mood for the day.

Citrus: Promotes productivity and calmness
Orange: Reduces anxiety
Vanilla: Strong relaxation effect
Peppermint: Boosts physical energy and alertness
Cedar: Reduces tension
Lavender: Promotes relaxation and sleep
Jasmine: Improves sleep and reduces anxiety
Rosemary: Improves long-term memory & boosts mood
Grapefruit: Increases energy
Lemon and Jasmine: Improves cognitive performance
Cinnamon and vanilla: Improves creativity
Frankincense: Reduces anxiety and depression
Rosemary and Grapefruit: boost long-term memory & energy
Ylang-Ylang: Reduces stress and promotes calmness
Lemon: Reduces stress and improves mood
Geranium plant: Reduces stress
Bergamot: Reduces anxiety
Chamomile flowers: Promotes calmness and relaxation
Valerian: Reduces anxiety & improves sleep
Chocolate: Increases theta brain waves & relaxation

Introduction to Magical Oils

The use of essential oils in magic and pagan traditions dates back to ancient times when natural remedies and spiritual practices were closely intertwined. Today, the enchanting properties of essential oils continue to play a vital role in modern-day witchcraft as practitioners seek to harness the power of nature to enhance their spells and rituals.

From promoting healing and relaxation to invoking love and prosperity, essential oils offer many magical benefits. Whether you're new to witchcraft or a seasoned practitioner, incorporating essential oils into your practice can help you connect with the natural world and tap into its limitless potential.

So if you're ready to explore the mystical world of essential oils and discover their potent properties for yourself, read on to learn more about the fascinating uses of these powerful plant extracts in magic and pagan traditions.

Spiritual Oil Properties

Uncrossing Oil

Uncrossing oil is used to shake off jinxes, hexes, and plain old bad luck. Being "crossed" means feeling magickally out of sorts. Being down on your luck, off your game, hitting a wall, losing your mojo—everybody knows what that feels like. Uncrossing magick is sometimes necessary to get the good vibes flowing again. Most Uncrossing Oils contain garden plants with high spiritual vibrations and a reputation for cleansing. Verbena, Hyssop (and its relative, Mint), Lavender, and Rose are common ingredients. Their aromas help break up stagnant energy patterns, impart a holy aura to places and people, and function as mood-lifters to get the magick back on track.

Van Van Oil

A traditional New Orleans Voodoo oil, Van Van is worn as a lucky all-purpose oil, protective ointment, and Bayou Witch's signature fragrance. It's hard to describe, but you will recognize it anywhere once you've smelled it. Says Cat Yronwode, "At one time, it is said, a person could not walk down a street in the Algiers district (of New Orleans) without smelling the scent of Van Van oil." Use it to anoint lucky charms and magickal tools. Dress candles. Cleanse and bless. Mix into floor washes and room sprays to banish negativity. Then, splash some into a cleansing bath to boost your mojo before doing any spell work.

Black Cat Oil

Black Cat Oil is another traditional New Orleans preparation. It is a lucky oil, particularly for witches, tricksters, charmers, and loners—that is, people of a feline nature. European tradition says a black cat is unlucky, but in Afro-American folk magick, black cats are considered good luck and the wise man or woman's helper. Use Black Cat Oil as an anointing oil to boost witchy powers and slip away from bad luck. Invisibility, enthrallment, clairvoyance, charisma—all fall into Black Cat magick's domain. Work Black Cat Oil spells during the waning or dark moon.

Abramelin Oil

The oldest recipe on this list, Abramelin Oil, appears in the late medieval grimoire The Book of the Sacred Magic of Abramelin the Mage. The 19th-century Hermetic Order of the Golden Dawn members later seized upon the formula. It appears in modern high magick traditions (notably Thelema) and has also trickled down into the altars of Pagan and folk-magick conjurors.

How to use Abramelin Oil: consecrating altar tools, evoking or communing with malevolent spirits, anointing the body for working high magick stuff. Abramelin Oil is highly stimulating and purifying. Applying to the brow or other chakras creates a warming sensation that enhances focus and energy flow for rituals.

Sabbat Oils

General Sabbat Oil

3 drops of frankincense oil
2 drops of myrrh oil
2 drops of sandalwood oil
1 drop of orange oil
1 drop of lemon oil

Yule Oil

2 drops of cinnamon oil
2 drops of clove oil
1 drop of mandarin oil
1 drop of pine oil
2 drops of frankincense oil
2 drops of myrrh oil

Imbolc Oil

2 drops of jasmine oil
2 drops of rose oil
2 drops of chamomile oil
2 drops of lemon oil
2 drops of lavender oil

Spring Equinox Oil

4 drops of lavender oil
2 drops of apple oil
2 drops of pear oil
2 drops of peach oil
1 drop of thyme oil
1 drop of marjoram oil
1 drop of elder oil

Beltane Oil

5 drops of rose oil
2 drops of dragon's blood
3 drops of coriander oil
(use almond oil as a base)

Midsummer Oil

4 drops of lavender oil
3 drops of rosemary oil
1 drop of pine oil
(use sunflower oil as your base)

Lughnasadh Oil

2 drops of peppermint oil
3 drops of elder oil
1 drop of fir oil
1 drop of hazelnut oil
(use corn oil as a base)

Mabon Oil

4 drops of rosemary oil
4 drops of frankincense oil
2 drops of apple oil
1 drop of chamomile oil
(use almond oil as a base)

Samhain Oil

3 drops of rosemary
3 drops of pine
3 drops of bay
3 drops of apple
2 drops of patchouli oil

Empath Suggestions

It's important to clear your energy each day by releasing any negative emotions, feelings, and energy. Spending time in nature and grounding yourself can also help maintain balance. Practicing meditation can assist in calming your emotions. Positive self-talk and affirmations are essential to maintain a healthy state of mind. Set boundaries, and don't be afraid to say "no" without an explanation. Engage in regular exercise to get rid of stagnant energy. Eating fruits and vegetables and drinking water can cleanse and rejuvenate you. Make sure you take some time for yourself to relax and get restorative sleep.

Let It Go Roll-On
5 drops of Sandalwood EO
3 drops Cypress EO
4 drops of Orange EO
2 drops of Grapefruit EO
5 ml of carrier oil of your choosing

Grounding Bath
15 drops of Ylang Ylang EO
2 cups of Epsom salt
A handful of Rose Petals
A handful of Dandelion Petals

Chill After-Bath Roller Blend
6 drops of Frankincense EO
8 drops of Vetiver EO
8 drops of Lemon EO
8 drops of Clary Sage EO

Happy House Diffuser Blend
2 drops of Chamomile EO
2 drops of Clary Sage EO
2 drops of Frankincense EO
2 drops of Bergamot EO
2 drops of Rose EO

Energy Clearing Spray
1 drop of Ylang ylang EO
1 drop of Cedarwood EO
2 drops of Angelica EO
2 drops of Pine EO
30 ml distilled water

Useful Herbs: Rose petals, chamomile, lavender, dandelion root, lemon balm, and skullcap

Summer Song Recipes

Shake It Off
5 drops of Lavender EO
4 drops of Ylang-ylang EO
3 drops of Tangerine EO

Don't Worry Be Happy
4 drops of Bergamot EO
2 drops of Grapefruit EO
2 drops of Lemon EO
2 drops Ylang-ylang EO

Sitting on the Dock of the Bay
5 drops of Frankenisenes EO
3 drops Rosemary EO
2 drops of Grapefruit EO
2 drops of Orange EO
1 drop of Eucalyptus EO

Summer Breeze
3 drops of Lemon EO
3 drops of Tangerine EO
3 drops of Grapefruit EO
1 drop of Cedarwood EO
1 drop of Jasmine EO

Itsy Bitsy Teenie Weenie
5 drops of Lemon EO
2 drops of Spearmint EO
1 drop of Basil

Summertime
5 drops of Bergamot EO
3 drops of Grapefruit EO
2 drops of Ylang-ylang EO

California Girls
4 drops of Spearmint EO
3 drops of Orange EO
2 drops of Geranium EO
2 drops of Lemon EO

Magical Essential Oil Recipes

Passion Oil
This may increase passionate feelings
1/2 part Rose
1/2 part Violet
1/2 part Ylang Ylang
2 drops of Saffron Extract
2 drops of Musk

I Love Me
This can be used to help bring out your inner goddess
1/2 part Rose
1/2 part Ylang Ylang
1/2 part Sandalwood
1/4 part Camphor
1/4 part Lemon

Retrograde Made Easy Oil
This can be used to release and let go of things that are holding you back.
1/2 part Lavender
1/2 part Lemon
3 drops of Bergamot
5 drops of Vetiver
5 drops of Lemongrass

Higher Energy Oil
This can be used to increase/lift your energy vibration
1/2 part Beargamot
1/4 part Orange
1/8 part Neroli
1/8 part Cinnamon

Introduction to Spells

Step into a world of secret enchantment with these concise and powerful witchy tips, granting you quick clarity for your magical path!

Throughout history, spells have fascinated humans as powerful rituals that can help them achieve their intentions and desires. In the world of magic and witchcraft, spells are carefully crafted using intention, symbolism, and energy manipulation to create change in the world. Spells can serve many purposes, such as attracting a romantic partner, inviting abundance, or warding off negative energies. They allow individuals to tap into their inner resources, connect with the energies of the universe, and manifest their desires in alignment with their highest good. Exploring the world of spells can open up new possibilities and reveal the mysteries of the metaphysical, where intention meets action.

Spells come in many forms, each with its unique focus, tools, and methods. From candle magic and herbal spells to sigil work and crystal enchantments, the world of spells offers a diverse array of approaches to manifesting change. While some spells draw upon ancient traditions and folklore, others are born from personal intuition and creativity. Some spells can be elaborate, incorporating intricate ingredients and rituals, while others can be as simple as a spoken affirmation or visualization. The beauty of exploring spells lies in their adaptability and personalization. Practitioners can find the methods and practices that resonate with them, infuse their spells with personal meaning and intention, as well as discover their own unique style of spellcasting. The world of spells is vast and ever-evolving, offering endless possibilities for those seeking to deepen their connection with magic and their own innate power.

Spell Jars

Anxiety Be-Gone Spell Jar
This can be used to help you feel calm and in control of your life
Lavender
Chamomile
Sage
Magical Water
Amethyst
And your petition on a bay leaf or paper wrapped around a bay leaf

Protection Spell Jar
Salt
White Rice
Common Sage
Lavender
Rosemary

Healing Spell Jar
Salt
Honey
Mint
Sunflower Petals
Agate
Amethyst

Cleansing Spray

Ingredients:
A Spray bottle
Sage
Rosemary
Sea Salt
Spring or rainwater
A couple of drops of lemon juice

Directions:
Boil the water and pour over the herbs and salt.
Leave covered until cool.
Strain and add to a dark spray bottle.
Add a couple of drops of lemon juice.

Use this spray to cleanse objects, people, or an area, just as you would use smudge sticks.

For a house, start from the corner furthest from the front door and work your way forward, making sure to get corners.

Energy Clearing Spray

Ingredients:
2 drops of palo santo EO
2 drops of sage EO
2 drops of bergamot EO
1 drop of lime EO
30 ml distilled water

Directions:
Use a 4oz spray bottle and fill most of the way with distilled water.
Add the EO's and shake well to mix.
Add a small chip of Amethyst or other protecting crystal of your choice.
Shake well before each use.

Use to clear a room of negative energy or spray your hands and arms before, during, and after energy sessions.

Freezer Binding Spell

Ingredients:
Piece of paper and a pen
Black thread or string
Small watertight container

Directions:
To protect yourself from harm, try writing the name of the person you wish to avoid on a piece of paper. Take a moment to visualize their face as vividly as possible. Afterward, fold the paper three times and tie it securely with black thread or string. Place the paper in a small, watertight container and fill it with water. Find a safe place to store the container, away from any potential disturbance, and say:

"Stay there, and freeze as long as I please."

Remember to renew the process every month or when the person starts bothering you again.

Harvest Blessing

Ingredients:
A small basket of fresh fruits or vegetables

Instructions:
Hold the basket of fruits or vegetables in your hands and visualize the energy of the harvest season. Feel gratitude for the abundance of the Earth and say:

"Lammas blessings, the harvest is here,
For the abundance we receive, I cheer.
With gratitude in my heart, I embrace this feast,
Nourished and blessed, my soul finds peace."

Types of Salt for Magic

Himalayan/Pink Salt ("purest salt on Earth" because of maturing for 250 million years)
Used for love, removing negative blockages & curses, and cleansing.

Hawaiian Black Salt (harvested from the evaporated water on Hawaiian Island Molokai) is used for its extra strength.

Table Salt
Used for purifying, protecting, and cleansing, and used in culinary recipes.

Kosher Salt (blessed by a Jewish rabbi)
Used to draw out negativity or absorbs negativity

Black Salt (leftover ashes or scrapings from cast iron)
Used for banishing and protection.

Alaea/Hawaiian Red Salt (From iron-rich volcanic clay)
Used for love and sex, blocks negative energy, protects aggressively to defend an area that has been set with or encircled with it, and is used in culinary recipes (high in nutrients 80+).

Sel Gris Sea Salt
Used for blessing.

Celtic Sea Salt
Used for protection and attracting financial abundance.

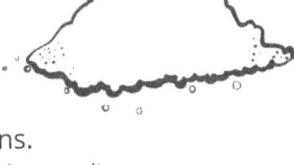

Sea Salt (carries the power of the sea and water elements)
Used for purification and cleansing, helps to balance emotions.

Cyprus Black Salt (sea water dried in lava beds mixed with charcoal)
Used to evoke properties of the pyramids, energy from heaven, used in culinary recipes.

Rock Salt
Used for return to sender, used to reflect negativity to sender.

Fleur de Sel Salt (sea salt from France)
Is a gentler salt used with fairies and elementals.

Gray Salt (developed in clay pools)
Used in liminal workings.

Blue Salt (sea salt mixed with blue flowers)
Used for protection from the Evil eye, justice, and healing.
That being said, you can make any color salt by mixing colored herbs with it.

Herb Infused Salts (salt infused with edible herbs)
Choose an herb that aligns with your intentions.

Epsom Salt
Use in the bath to reduce inflammation, muscle pain and to help you de-stress.

Pickling Salt (purest form, no added agents)
Used for purification, preservation of love, prosperity, etc., and used in culinary recipes.

Introduction to Manifestation

The process of manifestation involves turning your desires and intentions into reality through focused thought, belief, and action. It requires aligning your thoughts, emotions, and energy with the outcomes that you want to attract, resulting in positive changes in your life. Manifestation is based on the fundamental principle that our thoughts and beliefs can shape our reality. By consciously directing our thoughts and focusing our energy on what we wish to manifest, we can tap into the universal energy and co-create our desired outcomes. This powerful tool empowers individuals to actively participate in their own life's journey and harness the forces of the universe to manifest their dreams, goals, and aspirations. With intention, clarity, and faith, manifestation opens doors to limitless possibilities and brings about profound transformation and fulfillment.

Manifestation Mantras

I attract massive amounts of happiness.

I accept myself unconditionally.

I have plenty of time and energy to do the things I need to do.

All I need is within me.

I have enough. I do enough. I am enough.

I attract love, success, freedom, and health into my life.

My money is an unlimited resource and is constantly flowing my way.

My wildest dreams are coming true.

I am in the right place at the right time.

The Universe is bringing good things my way, and I am already thankful for them.

Magic will always surround me.

Opportunities will always come my way.

I can see the future that I want to have and know that it is on its way.

Manifestation Methods

3 6 9 Method
Write your desires 3 times in the present tense. Write your intention 6 times. Write the outcome 9 times.

Manifestation Meditation
Every spiritual person practices some form of meditation because it is how you connect with your higher power. Meditation allows divine wisdom and spiritual guidance to come through.

Manifestation Jar/Box
A manifestation jar is a container that holds all the desires you want to manifest. The things that you put into the jar represent your requests to the Universe, and anything you put in will manifest in your reality.

Manifestation Journal
A manifestation journal is a dedicated journal that you use with the intention of manifesting what you want into reality. Write about the goals and life that you want to attract.

Scripting
Scripting is a manifestation technique that involves describing the experience you would like to manifest as if it has already happened.

Gratitude
Be grateful for what you have right now. Manifestation happens when you're vibrating at a high frequency.

Subliminals
Subliminals can help you gently reprogram your subconscious mind by releasing the limiting beliefs that no longer serve you and filling them with new beliefs that do serve you.

The Pillow Method
Write your intention on a scrap of paper and tack it under your pillow. Then, every night, read what you've written and focus on it while falling asleep.

Visualization
Visualization helps you get into vibrational alignment with your desire by cultivating the feeling of experiencing your desire as if it has manifested.

55x5 Manifestation
Write your affirmation 55 times for 5 days to manifest your desire. This helps you become a vibrational match for what you want and attract it into your life.

Manifestation Notes:

Warding

Warding is a form of defensive magic that offers a gentle approach to protection. Its purpose is to safeguard against negative energies, redirecting them away from you or your surroundings in a general sense.

Methods

Guardians
Create a guardian to guard your home or space against negative energies.

Crystals
Corresponding crystals can be worn on jewelry to protect against negative energy. Place crystals in a room or around your house to create a protective barrier.

Salt
Black salt can be used in rituals or just used alone. Sprinkle salt around your doors and windows, or make protection jars with it.

Herbs
Burn protective herbs and pass the smoke through your space or tools. Sprinkle herbal oils and tinctures on yourself and your space for protective barriers.

Visualization
Use your intention and energy to visualize a powerful barrier of protecting light around yourself or your space.

Trust your instincts and rely on methods that resonate with you. Avoid using techniques that don't feel right or that you haven't thoroughly researched.

Spell for Warding

Ingredients:
- Small white candle
- Protection herbs (e.g., rosemary, basil, sage)
- Protective crystals (e.g., black tourmaline, obsidian, clear quartz)
- Sea salt
- Anointing oil (e.g., olive or coconut oil)
- Fire-safe bowl or cauldron

Instructions:
1. Clear and prepare your sacred space. Light a white candle.
2. Crush protection herbs and roll the white candle in anointing oil. Coat the candle in crushed herbs.
3. Place a circle of protective crystals around the candle and sprinkle sea salt in a circle around them.
4. Light the white candle and state your warding intention.
5. Visualize a protective shield forming around you and your space.
6. Let the candle burn down completely in a safe manner.
7. Express gratitude and close your sacred space.

Banishing

Regarding defensive magic, banishing is a much more targeted and forceful approach than warding. Its purpose is to eliminate a specific energy, spirit, or individual. However, it's essential to carefully consider the consequences before resorting to banishing.

Methods

Use the Elements
Burn a slip of paper with your target's name on it or throw a leaf with your target's name on it in a running river/stream. Burn corresponding herbs and pass the smoke through your space.

Candles
Anoint your candle with corresponding herbs and oils, then burn it when the candle has burnt out; the banishing is complete.

Sigils
Make your own banishing sigil, or find one that resonates with you; place it in the space or on the item you are banishing energy from.

Herbs & Tinctures
Use herbal smoke to force energy out of a space or object; make a spray or herbal tincture to sprinkle around your home.

Trust your instincts and rely on methods that resonate with you. Avoid using techniques that don't feel right or that you haven't thoroughly researched.

Spell for Banishing

Ingredients:
Small black candle
Pinch of sea salt
Handful of dried sage leaves
Piece of paper
Black pen or marker
Fire-safe bowl or cauldron

Instructions:
Clear and prepare your sacred space.
Write down what you want to banish on the piece of paper.
Place the black candle in the center and sprinkle a pinch of sea salt around it.
Light the black candle and recite your banishing incantation.
Hold sage leaves over the flame to smolder and let the smoke surround you.
Visualize the negative energies leaving and into the flame.
Burn the paper and affirm your release from what you wish to banish.
Let the candle burn out safely.
Bury or scatter the cooled ashes.
Express gratitude and close your sacred space.
Remember to approach the spell with respect, focus, and sincere intentions for positive change.

Introduction to Crossroads

Crossroads hold a mystical allure and have been steeped in magical significance across various cultures and belief systems. Symbolically, a crossroads represents a point of convergence, where paths intersect and choices are made. It is a liminal space where the veil between worlds is believed to be thin, granting access to spiritual realms and unseen forces. Crossroads are considered potent locations for rituals, spells, and divination in magical practices. They are seen as places of power where one can seek guidance, make offerings, or connect with deities and spirits. Crossroads are also associated with transitions, transformation, and decision-making. They serve as gateways for releasing the old and embracing the new, making them ideal for spells related to change, protection, and opening new opportunities. Whether invoking the energies of Hecate at a three-way crossroad or burying an intention at a four-way crossroad, these magical junctions hold the potential for deep spiritual connections and profound personal growth.

Leave

Things to leave at the crossroads for power or ritual.

Offerings
Spiritual offerings and prayers can be left at the crossroads to show thanks or strengthen your relationships with spirits. Be sure to leave appropriate offerings for the particular spirits you are working with or for the specific prayer/work.

Active Spells
The crossroads is a perfect place to anchor spells related to the power of that crossroads. Burying a spell designed to work long term here will allow the work to stay strong and progress without being actively worked at home.

Spell Remains
Most spellwork remains can be buried, burned, or left at the crossroads. This brings their energy to full completion. It lets any leftover prayer or intent in the plants, petitions, or other remains of the work be fully and safely released. Use mindfully.

Take

Things to take from the crossroads for spells or charms.

Dirt
Crossroads dirt brings the power of manifestation from the crossroads. Dirt from male crossroads is excellent to manifest customers to a business. Dirt from a divine crossroads mixed into a garden or field attracts good spirits and increases harvest.

Stones
Crossroads stones carry the power of the crossroads itself with them. Pregnant women can carry stones from a female crossroads to protect the baby.
Stones from damned crossroads may be left in a house, yard, or field to curse it and make it barren.

Coins
Coins found at the crossroads are especially powerful. Silver coins found here protect from haunting nightmares and evil spirits. Copper coins protect one who carries them from love spells and binding. You may leave coins on purpose to pick up later but found is always best.

Cemetery vs. Graveyard

What's a Cemetery?
A cemetery is a place where people are buried. They are not associated with a church, so they are often larger as they can spread out beyond land adjacent to a church. Both religious and non-religious people can be buried there.

The word cemetery dates back to the late 14th century. However, its roots can be traced to the Old French word "cimetiere," derived from the Medieval Latin "cemeterium." Its literal translation is "a place set aside for the burial of the dead."

What's a Graveyard?
A graveyard, like a cemetery, is where people are buried after death. Graveyards are affiliated with a church and are typically located on church grounds. They tend to be smaller due to land limitations and, thus, are often exclusive. Only members of their religion and sometimes only members of that specific Church can be buried in a graveyard.

The origin of the word graveyard is somewhat straightforward. It is, after all, a yard filled with graves. It is interesting to note, though, that the word "grave" is derived from a proto-Germanic word "graban," which means "to dig."

People are buried in graveyards; in a cemetery, it is possible to bury an individual's ashes. When Christians talk about "holy ground," it is typically about a church building where God's presence is most keenly felt. While that may be true, one holy place that is often neglected is the local cemetery.

The Church has always treated the dead with the utmost respect; the cemetery is where that belief is practiced. For example, when a new Catholic cemetery is created, the bishop (or sometimes a priest appointed by him) will come out to bless it and hallow the ground where the dead will be buried. The first action of the bishop is to walk around the entire cemetery, sprinkling holy water on the earth.

Know the Rules

Graveyard

There are mundane rules and occult rules for working in cemeteries. But first, let's cover the ordinary rules. These will usually be posted at the entrance, especially in newer and commercially maintained burial grounds.

Graveyard visiting hours are important to consider for any Witch. Unfortunately, these hours are usually unposted and governed by state laws or local ordinances. Knowing these laws is important, as many cemeteries require you to leave at sundown. Violating these rules can result in various penalties, from being asked to leave to being arrested. So please respect the dead and the grieving, and observe all rules and regulations.

The magickal rules can be quite complicated. We don't know much about death, so we've had to make up many superstitions over the years. As a result, there are now many different beliefs surrounding graveyard visits. Here are some cool ones: Don't point at graves or photograph them. (this rule probably gets broken the most).

Say "sorry" when stepping over a gravesite (observed 100% of the time in Irish cemeteries and taught to me as a child).

It is bad luck to wear anything new to a cemetery, especially shoes.

Don't whistle in a graveyard, or you tempt Death!

Leaving coins on a grave is a token of respect.

Don't yawn near a grave, or ghosts could enter your body.

Smelling roses when there are none around is a sign that a benevolent spirit is nearby.

The person who takes something from a graveyard will return more than he took.

Working in cemeteries requires more than a little occult wisdom to master the art of magick. Each graveyard has its own unique energy, spirits, and customs – so it's hard to know what rules apply to every situation. But one universal truth remains: respect must always be shown - otherwise, your work will likely meet with resistance or, even worse... unpleasant consequences! Paying proper homage demonstrates reverence towards our dearly departed, allowing practitioners access to magical realms that would remain out of reach without due deference.

I Got a Jar of Dirt!

Types of Dirt and Their Magical Uses

Graveyard
Traditionally used in divination, cursing, love & protection spells
Avoid collecting from an unclean spirit's grave for most workings
Leave an offering in exchange for the dirt
Try to collect from an ancestor's grave to ensure the energy you are collecting is safe.

Churchyard
Traditionally used for many intentions and spells:
Healing
Prosperity
Purification
Protection
Mending relationships
Justice workings

Crossroad
They are traditionally used in road-opening spells
Used in journeying to the underworld, as it helps open the gate to the other realms
Used as offerings to guardians and gods of the crossroads: Hecate, Hermes, Papa Legba, etc.

Backyard
Traditionally used in workings for the family, home, and property:
Purification
Protection
Peace
Collect from the 4 corners of the property if possible.

Self-Care

Taking care of oneself should be a top priority, as no one can provide the same level of care as you can for yourself. Ignoring personal self-care can negatively impact both physical and emotional health and overall quality of life.

One can practice meditation in various forms, even just by engaging in deep breathing exercises for a few minutes. Focusing on the present moment and avoiding dwelling on the past or worrying about the future can be mentally beneficial.

Forgiving oneself and choosing love can help release past burdens and trauma while also acknowledging personal struggles. Letting go of judgment and choosing inner peace over conflict can lead to greater long-term satisfaction and emotional well-being. Opting for the high road in difficult situations can also test one's character and build resilience.

I possess the ability to release any burdensome thoughts or emotions that may be hindering me. Additionally, I make a conscious effort to forgive myself and refrain from self-criticism.

One of my top priorities is to nurture a sense of gratitude by purposefully acknowledging and expressing appreciation for the individuals and blessings in my life. By doing so, I am able to swiftly overcome any negative emotions that may arise.

It is always advisable to prioritize your happiness over being right when faced with situations that could compromise it. To achieve inner peace and tranquility, exploring spirituality can be of great help. Keeping an open heart and mind is vital in discovering the spiritual path that suits you best. Trusting your intuition is a natural ability that can positively transform your life. With a little faith, you can tap into its potential and gain empowerment.

I hope that you find happiness, peace, and love in your journey toward becoming the best possible version of yourself.

Self-Care Notes

Self-Care Affirmations

Self-Care Gratitude

Journal Prompts for Self-Reflection

Reflecting on your life and exploring your thoughts and emotions can be aided by using journaling prompts. They can bring clarity and understanding to your experiences while providing a safe space for you to express yourself without fear of judgment.

The versatility of journaling prompts is one of their greatest benefits. You can customize them to meet your unique needs and interests and use them to explore any aspect of your life. Whether you're interested in your relationships, career goals, personal values, or simply gaining a better understanding of yourself, there's a prompt suitable for you. You're free to choose the prompts that resonate with you and follow your authentic path.

Remember, there are no right or wrong answers when it comes to self-reflection. This is a personal journey, and the insights you gain are unique to you. Embrace the process, trust your intuition, and allow yourself to be vulnerable. Your journaling practice will evolve over time, and each entry will bring you closer to a deeper connection with yourself.

Self-Reflections

What does happiness mean to you?

Self-Reflections

At this moment, what are four things you're grateful for?

Self-Reflections

What are 10 things you love about yourself? Why?

Self-Reflections

How can I take better care of myself?

Self-Reflections

How can you feel more fulfilled in your life?

Self-Reflections

What activities sets your soul on fire?

Self-Reflections

What actions can you take today to simplify your life?

Self-Reflections

Write down your top 10 goals to complete by the end of the year.

Self-Reflections

How have you changed in the last 5 years?

Self-Reflections

Describe in great detail what 5 years from now looks like.

Notes

Notes

Notes

Notes

Notes

Index

12 Chakras..... 88

Acknowledgments..... 6

Angels..... 134

Animal Guides 126

App Recommendations..... 289

Archetypes..... 104

Astrological Signs..... 43

Auras..... 79

Banishing..... 253

Book Recommendations..... 287

Centering 93

Chakra Symbols..... 86

Chakras at a Glance..... 85

Chakras Energy.....84

Colors at First Glance..... 77

Correspondence..... 137

Crystals..... 186

Days Explained..... 36

Days for Spells and Rituals..... 35

Evil Eye Colors..... 120

Foraging Calendar 138

Goddesses..... 19

Gods..... 21

Grab and Go Combos..... 215

Grounding..... 89

Herbs..... 139

Index..... 280

Intro to Deities 18

Intro to Oils 231

Intro to Spells..... 243

Intro to Symbols..... 119

Intro to Tarot..... 49

Lughnasadh Around the World.....27

Lughnasadh at a Glance..... 14

Magic of the Months..... 48

Magical Water 224

Manifestation..... 249

Moons of the Year..... 32

Oh Crap, A Full Moon..... 30

Phases of the Moon..... 29

Quarter & Cross-Quarters..... 12

Quicky Lughnasadh..... 15

Correspondence..... 16

Runes..... 135

Sabbat Dates..... 8

Sabbats: Wheel of the Year..... 9

Self Care and Reflections..... 260

Self Healing Your Chakras..... 97

Shielding..... 95

Simplified Psychic Abilities..... 100

Spirituality..... 108

The Elements..... 109

The Moon and Lunacy..... 31

The Wheel Explained..... 10

Times for Spells and Rituals..... 40

Types of Empaths..... 101

Types of Spirit Guides..... 124

Using a Pendulum..... 98

Warding..... 251

What is a Spirit Guide..... 123

Wheel of the Year..... 7

Witch Words..... 106

Witchcraft Paganism Wicca..... 13

Witchy Services and Shops..... 282

Ying/Yang Energy..... 82

I just wanted to express my deepest gratitude for your unwavering support. It has been an absolute joy to share this journey with you, and I hope you've enjoyed it even half as much as I have. Every single like, follow, share, and review means the world to me. If you're feeling particularly generous, I would be truly moved if you could take a moment to spread the word about my books by leaving an honest review. Together, we can make this world a brighter, better place. Thank you from the bottom of my heart for everything.

Thank you!!
Robin

Mystic Mind Community

Why Join The Mystic MindCommunity?

We bring together spiritual people who are seeking more connection, the ability to share their own experiences, and learn from online Challenges, Live Events, Courses, and each other!

The concept for building this Spiritual Social Network is so we can grow together in a supportive, inclusive, and fun Spiritual Metaverse covering a wide range of spiritual resources.

The Mystic Mind Podcast

The Mystic Mind Podcast is a creative exploration to help support you in your intuitive and spiritual development journey and add a little fun!

I mean, we have to have fun on this journey, right?

As a professional Energy Healer and Spiritual Teacher, I share some of what I've learned along the way during my spiritual development journey for over a decade. In this podcast, you will find shows on Intuitive Development and/or reflections, Angels, Divination, Energy Work, special guests, interviews, and more.

Also, have you joined our Mystic Mind Community?
Mystic Mind PodcastAvailable on
Spotify
Anchor.fm
Amazon Music

Apple Music

DCNW Podcast:
Spotify:

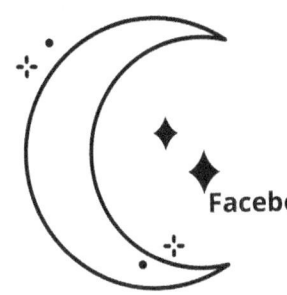

Colby Parrish

(727) 831-8077

Facebook: The Wondering Fool - Spiritual Advisor
Instagram: Thewonderingfool333
TikTok: TheWonderingFool333

Hours of Availability
Tuesday through Saturday 11 am - 8 pm EST

Service Menu
General Psychic Readings
30 min/$60
45min/$90
60min/$120

Tarot - Oracle - Lithomancy
3 Card Single Message
Pull/ $20
Couples Readings
40min/$80
Personal Monthly
Forecast/$120
Numerological
Chart/$150

Available for private parties and events!

He is my spiritual adviser, so I highly recommend him and his services!

Jamie Wareham

www.lightworkerpath.com
Email: lightworkerpathsite@gmail.com

Service Menu
Reiki + Sound Healing Sessions
Soul Coaching Sessions (spiritual life coaching)
Intuitive Development
Mentorship Programs
Reiki Level 1,2 & 3 Attunement
Certification Courses
Spiritual/Energy Development Classes

She is a fellow writer who co-authored "The Voyage & The Return: The Path to Self Discovery." Moreover, I've taken her classes, and they were interesting and helpful. She's super knowledgeable about energy work, angel spirit guides, meditation, and reiki healing.

Here is a profound quote from her book "Some of the best teachers are ones who have journeyed into the heart of darkness and come through it all like the powerful Phoenix they are! A rebirth into something else, something stronger, something that yearns to help others through their own forms of darkness."

Whimsical Cauldron and Crafts

www.whimsicalcauldronandcrafts.com
Email: Whimsicalcauldron2019@gmail.com
Facebook: Whimsical Cauldron and Crafts, LLC

They sell crystals, minerals, specimens, jewelry, herbs, sage, etc.
They also feature other vendors and their merchandise.

I have purchased almost everything they have for sale and can confidently say they are a great small business for high-quality crystal needs. They have always been kind and patient, especially when I first learned about crystals. If they didn't have something I was looking for, they would get it for me.

Third Eye Creations

www.fromthirdeye.com

Third Eye Creations is a great place to buy unique and exciting gifts. They have a storefront in The Marketplace of Tarpon Springs, Florida, including a magickal apothecary, a DIY Candle bar, and their online shop. You can also find their products at local businesses around the area.

Sabbat Boxes by Third Eye Creations! These amazing subscription boxes contain everything you need to honor each sabbat on the Wheel of the Year, with multiple items tailored to each celebration. And let's talk about the quality of these goodies - simply breathtaking! From spell candles with amazing scents and clean burning to tub teas perfect for spells, Third Eye Creations has it all. Don't miss out on the ultimate sabbat experience - get your Sabbat Box today! Plus, check out the witch kits and other awesome products available.

Emerald Coast Alternatives

emeraldcoastalternatives.com

Welcome to Emerald Coast Alternatives, your online herbal tea shop. We aim to provide accessible, effective, and affordable herbal tea blends that help you feel better and enjoy life more. Our teas are delicious and effective in managing symptoms of anxiety, PTSD, PMS, insomnia, inflammation, and headaches. We donate one Herbal Tea "Care Package" monthly to a Recovery Center in the USA. Thank you for choosing Emerald Coast Alternatives as your trusted herbal teas and self-healing tools source.

Follow them and learn more about what their products can provide on TikTok @freespirit.beauTEA

Enhance your Health with The Plant Cemetery Herbal Subscription Box!
MONTHLY HERBAL HEALTH & BEAU-TEA SUBSCRIPTION BOX
$10 OFF YOUR FIRST BOX with Code: PlantBox10
FREE SHIPPING ON ALL PRODUCTS!

Although I am not typically a tea fan, I absolutely adore the tea from this company. I purchase it frequently and have even signed up for their monthly subscription box.

Book Recommendations

I've compiled a list of books that I found informative and helpful. However, choosing which ones you want to read is ultimately up to you based on your goals, taste, and path. But I hope you find this list helpful and a great starting point.

Almanac in all forms

The Altar Within by Juliet Diaz

Penczak Temple Series by Christopher Penczak

Cunningham's Encyclopedia of Magical Herbs (Llewellyn's Sourcebook Series) (Cunningham's Encyclopedia Series, 1) by Scott Cunningham

The Green Witch: Your Complete Guide to the Natural Magic of Herbs, Flowers, Essential Oils, and More by Arin Murphy-Hiscock

Psychic Witch: A Metaphysical Guide to Meditation, Magick & Manifestation by Mat Auryn

Protection and Reversal Magick: A Witch's Defense Manual (Beyond 101) by Jason Miller

Year of the Witch: Connecting with Nature's Seasons through Intuitive Magick by Temperance Alden

Encyclopedia of Witchcraft by Judika Illes

The Ultimate Guide to Tarot Card Meanings by Brigit Esselmont

The Essential Guide to Crystals, Minerals, and Stones by Margaret Ann Lembo

Edible Wild Plants: Eastern/Central North America (Peterson Field Guides) by Roger Tory Peterson
but pretty much all the Peterson Field Guides

Backwoods Witchcraft: Conjure & Folk Magic from Appalachia by Jake Richards

Roots, Branches & Spirits: The Folkways & Witchery of Appalachia by H. Byron Ballard

Honoring Your Ancestors: A Guide to Ancestral Veneration by Mallorie Vaudoise

Book Recommendations

Magickal Mediumship by Daniell Dionne

Maximize 365 by Kristin A. Sherry

Knot Magic by Sarah Bartlett

Encyclopedia of Spirits by Judika Illes

Answering the Call of the Elementals by Thomas Mayer

The Twelve Faces of the Goddess by Danielle Blackwood

The Universe is Talking to You by Tammy Mastroberte
Llewellyn's Practical Magic Series

Modern Witchcraft Series by Skye Alexander

Brigit Esselmont Books

Elements of Witchcraft Series

Apps I am Researching/Researched

My Moon Phase
Moonly
Co-Star
Stellarium Mobile - Star Map
Stars and Planets
Globe 3D - Planet Earth
Star Registration - Night Sky
Solar Walk Lite Planetarium 3D
Labyrinthos
Crystal Gemstones
PictureThis
Growit
WiccaCalendar
TheCornellLab
Cafe Astrology.com
Horoscope
Sigilscribe.me
Headspace
InsightTimer
Down Dog
Audible/Kindle/Kindle Unlimited

Websites

OtherworldlyOracle.com
The.mindsjournalJournal.com
oneessentialcommunity.com
herbal-supplement-resource.com
greenwitchlivingofficial.com
thepeculiarbrunette.com

Facebook Groups

I have found some valuable information from
Otherworldly Oracle Group Facebook Group
The Modern Empath
Spiritual Alchemists - A Group For The Spiritually Curious

Discover a world of possibilities at KIPS Publishing LLC. Books have the power to transform lives and expand horizons. And we are proud to bring you some of the most captivating, informative, and inspiring books you can imagine. Now, with just one scan of our QR code, you can access a whole library of books from KIPS and discover the best of what we have to offer. So take advantage of this exciting opportunity to take your reading journey to the next level. Scan now and open the doors to a world of knowledge, imagination, and inspiration!

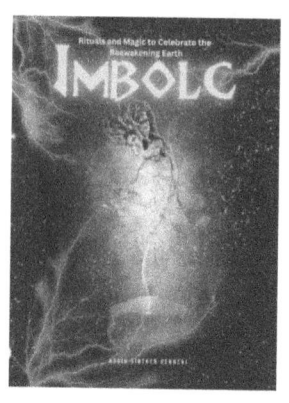

 Scan here for the latest release
from Robin Ginther Venneri
and KIPS Publishing

Thank you so much for your support!

If you enjoyed this book, then kindly leave a review on Amazon and on any of your social media accounts, and please tag me on them.

Blessings to You and Yours,
Robin Ginther-Venneri

Questions, concerns, and ideas can be directed to KIPSPublishingllc@gmail.com.

How to Support Indie (Independent) Authors:

Review their books:
Like & comment on their posts:
Share their in-story or about pages:
Preorder their books. You know you are going to buy them anyway!
Recommend them to other readers:
Email or message about a book of theirs you loved:
Follow them on social media.